THE ATTRACTIVE PRACTICE MODEL FOR CHIROPRACTORS

Proven systems to increase clients, get better results, maximise income and increase time-off

Mark Postles D.C.

ISBN (Ebook) 978-0-6456960-0-4
ISBN (Paperback) 978-0-6456960-1-1

Edited by Clare McIvor (Clare McIvor Writing and Communications)
Layout and Design by AsiaType
Illustrations by Quest Transformative Services

Contents

Introduction

Steve Jobs said, "The most powerful person in the world is the story-teller. The storyteller sets the vision, values and agenda of an entire generation that is to come." Dr Mark Postles is a storyteller, but more, he is a disciple of the discipline of detailed implementation. After all, what good is a vision, a story, if it is not actualized? Famed social scientist and leadership guru, Warren Bennis, defined leadership as a formula of *vision and power*. He defined *vision* as the ability to give an individual or an organization an image of its potential that's greater than the vision it holds on its own. He defined *power* as the skill of being able to transform that vision into reality. In The Attractive Practice Model (TAPM), Mark accomplishes both.

TAPM begins with the most vital factor in business success, *you*. After having built the largest practice management program ever in chiropractic, coached more than 10,000 chiropractors, been the President of the original Chiropractic College and the Chancellor of the largest Chiropractic College in the world, I'm confident in stating the size, impact and growth of a business is directly related to what's on the inside of a human being. First you *be* then you *do* and the result is what you *have*. *Be-Do-Have* and it doesn't happen any other way. Mark knows and lives this formula and hence teaches this principle of success.

The first chapter is about who you *be*, *The Attractive Character*, which then evolves to *doing*, the writing of a *power purpose and values statement* (very Disney-like, btw) along with dynamic procedures, and TAPM culminates in *lasting legacy* and success.

I believe strongly that for our profession to flourish we have to have skill and competency in 5 critical arenas.

Our chiropractic colleges must turn out skilled and knowledgeable new grads in the disciplines of philosophy, neurology and clinical care.

We need motivated/committed practice management programs to mould the new grad into a business person with the discipline of empathetic care for their practice members.

The individual practitioner is, of course, the cornerstone of the profession, because it is here that the vision of chiropractic is realized in adding millions of healthier years to millions of healthier humans.

Select individuals must be willing to take on the added professional responsibility of local/state association activity and politics to protect our profession and ensure equitable access for the public.

The CVO (Chief Vision Officer)...the Storyteller who sets the vision and agenda for this and coming generations is vital to a purposeful profession..

Mark has played all of these roles at one time or another in his career. It's probably why he is so loved and revered in Australia-New Zealand. Remarkably, he has advanced our profession from pre-licensure to government recognition of chiropractic; he was at the core of developing and guiding chiropractic education from the onset; he managed and taught along with his faithful partner, Jackie, Renaissance and Quest to prepare new chiropractors for success; he's been involved with the politics of chiropractic; and, finally, he has always set the vision and a course for the future for our profession.

There is no one more prepared to write a book of this importance and no one I am more proud to call a colleague and friend.

Dr. Guy Riekeman

Entrepreneur and Chancellor Emeritus, Life University

Foreword

It was September 2001, imagine a room filled with exuberant chiropractors, the alcohol was flowing and the band was blasting hit after hit, the dance floor was full, dinner had not even been served. It was not long before the auction started, and hands were flying and money was being spent. The following day a little less exuberant, we discovered we were the lucky recipients of some chiropractic coaching with Mark Postles. This was the beginning of an incredible journey of self and professional discovery, building our chiropractic dream practice and many wonderful life lessons along the way.

Mark is now a close friend, and someone who is incredibly dear to our hearts. We are not alone, as Mark has this incredible ability to see the good and possibility in everyone. His dedication to the chiropractic profession and ensuring that it flourishes is all part of what makes Mark brilliant.

We, like so many others have been inspired to serve in greater ways for the betterment of the profession. Ash served 17 years on the Board of Trustees for the New Zealand College of Chiropractic, and chaired the board for the last 8 of these. With encouragement and support from Mark I stepped into the role of Dean of Chiropractic at the New Zealand College of Chiropractic for four years. These roles have all been about keeping sacred and helping to keep chiropracTIC strong and flourishing in the world. Meanwhile we have served in our own dream attractive practice for the last 20 years in Glen Eden, Auckland. Where we have worked with Mark and Quest to implement the vital aspects of what it takes to build an attractive practice. This has formed the foundation of our attractive practice from a cultural, team, systems and growth perspective. The process works so well, that we were able to step out of our practice for a year with our young children and travel the world, meanwhile the practice thrived in our absence.

How to build an Attractive Practice gives the reader a strong foundation upon which to build their own attractive practice. It challenges the status quo, and encourages the reader to shed your old archaic views on practice building to adopt a more sustainable and joyful approach. This approach is congruent with both chiropractic principles and human nature. It helps the reader to understand themselves first and by doing so they are better equipped to connect with others as they build better teams, practice, and systems. A strong and consistent theme throughout the book is the in8model® which serves to demonstrate traits, characteristics, preferences, procedures and systems. The in8model® explains the ever-evolving nature of practice, and offers solutions to help you grow and expand your thinking and thrive. The end result being untold success in practice, fun, engaged and efficient teams, constant growth which leads to financial freedom.

Even after 20 years in the same practice we read this book and have gained some remarkable insights to current challenges, and it has been inspired to think about what is next. If going to practice and feeling fulfilled, joyful and on purpose is what you want, whilst being financially rewarded for your service this is the book for you.

Thank you Mark for your dedication to the chiropractic profession, for always questing for excellence in yourself and for all of us.

Drs Katie and Ash Pritchard

Welcome to the
Attractive Practice MODEL

This book is for you if you are the Chiropractor who is looking to create a sustainable and philosophically congruent practice that is attractive to your ideal people. The result is that they will pay, stay and refer others for a lifetime.

In your unique way, you will consume the content and context of this book in your preferred method. I have laid it out in a way in which you will get the most from it.

As your practice is an evolving, living organism, you will find yourself referencing different Quadrants in the book to help scale your practice through to being a viable business.

The context of this book is framed around the function of the human brain as described in the in8model®. You will notice that each process and procedure is based on this in8model® structure, so you'll get used to the in8model® diagram popping up, demonstrating the topic in hand.

The content is broken into segments that give a rationale for the topic, examples of it, a description of it, followed by a Playtime section with a few to-dos and a Summary of the key points of the topic. Depending on your Quadrant preferences, you may find that one of these aspects is your happy place for getting the most from the read.

Use the links to our resources which are placed in QR Codes at relevant places to get more information of a given topic and make sure that you call out to us if you wish to get greater clarity on any subject.

There are 3 models that we refer to continually throughout this book. They are best viewed in colour so I have placed them together here at the beginning of the book.

The Attractive Practice Model is an adaptation of the brain-based in8model®. In this book, we explore eight in8model® strategies shown here.

The 8 Strategies Of The Attractive Practice Model

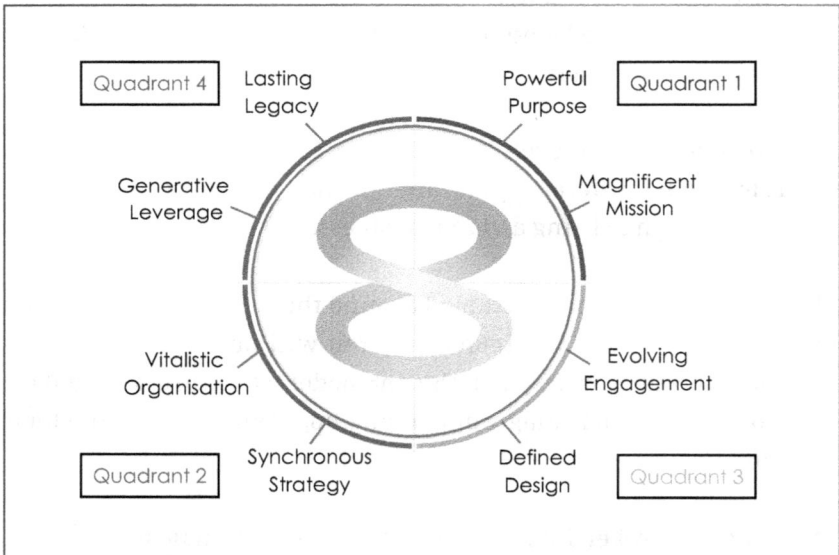

Quadrant 4	Lasting Legacy	Powerful Purpose	Quadrant 1
	Generative Leverage	Magnificent Mission	
	Vitalistic Organisation	Evolving Engagement	
Quadrant 2	Synchronous Strategy	Defined Design	Quadrant 3

The metaphor that we use to guide practice members through their clinical experience is the Journey as shown here.

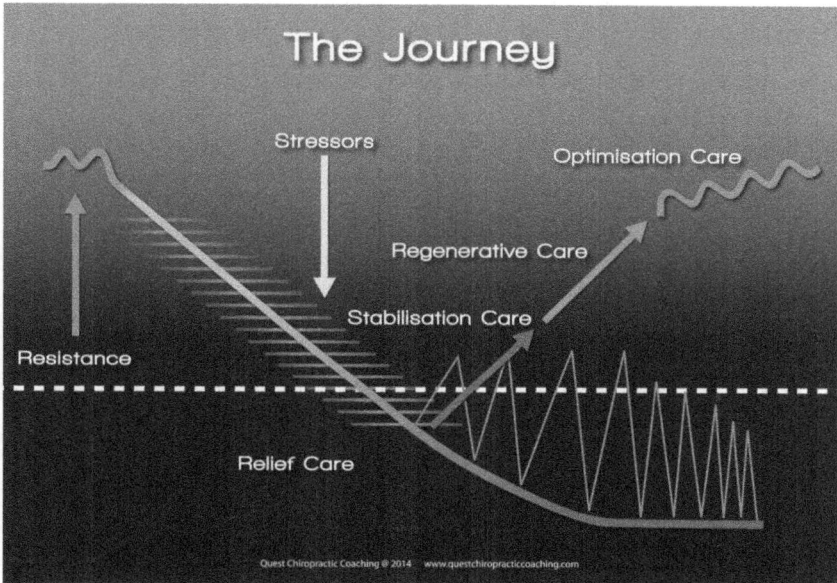

THE VOYAGE CHART

The Voyage

PV /Month	Income /Month	Income /Year	ATTRACT	NURTURE	DELIVER	EXPAND
1500	87,000	$1 mil+	• Curiosity • The Next Iteration • Collaborative Partnerships	• Operations Manager • Publish • Scientific Contribution	• Optimisation of Resources • Clinical Contribution to Profession • Wayshower Governance	• Political Influence • Growing Legacy • Equity Sell-Offs
1300	75,400	$900k	• Completion • Generative Sessions • Patterns	• Impact on Profession • Playing the Long Game • Board of Directors	• Branded by Technique • Chiropractic Finishing School • Internal Mentoring	• Multiple Income Streams • Compensation • Business Model 301
1100	63,800	$760k	• Community • Congruence • Events Driven Practice	• Profitability • Team Empowerment • in8model - Associates	• Team Ascension • Executive Assistant • Personal Care - 301	• Communication - 301 • Financial Contribution • Recurring Income
900	52,200	$625k	• Redesign • PM Ascension • Attracting Associates	• Practice Layout • Associate Driven Practice • OPM - Expand	• Transferable Protocols • Contact Hours/% of Income • Personal Care - 201	• Free Up A DAy • Investment Strategies • Seeding Practices
700	40,600	$490k	• Communication 201 • Cultivating Chiropractors • Team Centered Mission	• Debt Reduction • Operational Cascade • OPM -Deliver	• Time & Motion • Meetings that Matter • Tech CA	• Statistics • Wealth Building • Business Model 201
500	29,000	$350k	• Physical Marketing • Culture • Client Centered Mission	• 3rd Phase - Optimisation Care • in8model - Business • OPM - Nurture	• Educational Plan • Internal Referrals • Personal Care 101	• Default Diary • Holidays • Congruence
300	17,400	$210k	• Annual Marketing Plan • The Journey - QPFLTC • Automated Lead Generation	• 2nd Phase - Regenerative Care • Storyboards • OPM - Attract	• Clinical Clarity • State Control • Communication - 101	• The Super CA • Management • Business Model 101
200	11,600	$140k	• Purpose, Outcomes • Bay 5 - Mission • Bay 1 - Beliefs	• 1st Phase - Stabilisation Care • Bay 6 - Strategy • Bay 2 - Organisation	• Visits 1&2 • Bay 7 - Design • Bay 3 - Engagement	• Money • Bay 8 - Leverage • Bay 4 - Empowerment

* Based on per visit of $58

The coaching model we take our Questers (Quest coaching clients) on is called the The Voyage as shown above.

Preface

Retention. When I think of that word, I think of 'forcibly holding something back'. I think of fluid retention, lymph retention, or anal retention. I think of water in a pond, stagnating because it is not flowing and moving or fresh.

That is how my practice was at one point. Once the practice member had been attracted to the practice and 'converted' to care, I found myself working hard to hold onto them. *This* was retention in practice.

It was not what I wanted. I got into my profession because I wanted to serve people who wanted to evolve. I wanted to attend to empowered people, to journey with them and to be the observer of their life's enrichment for as long as I was useful.

My lessons in growing practices over the years have shown me that the fundamental structure determines the outcome. I was brought up in my very early days in the profession with the notion that I had to hustle, to push and pull patients into the practice. I used all sorts of tricks and tactics, from putting on the attractive face, and using super offers, discounts, and enticements all geared to getting people in the door. Don't get me wrong. I was doing it from an intense passion for the value of my offering. It was driven by a desire for others to have access to the wonders of Chiropractic.

When they came in, I eagerly focused on converting them to my way of thinking so I could turn them into lifetime clients. Conversion was tricky at best. It was frustrating work for me and annoying for the potential practice member who felt that they were being sold to.

Several years into practice, I started questioning this mindset of attraction, conversion and retention. In 1977 my thinking was massively expanded by my mentors, Dr Joseph Flesia and Dr Guy Riekeman who brought their Renaissance program (which later became the Quest Alliance) to Australia and New Zealand. The global vision of the impact of Chiropractic expressed by these two warriors lit a flame for me and we have flown the Quest flag ever since.

One day, a practice member mentioned that she had visited the practice for over 900 visits. Cheekily, I asked her why she would spend that much time and money in coming in to be cared for by us. Her simple response was "because this practice is attractive in so many ways–I just love everything about it. I am a better person because of Chiropractic". This got me thinking. Really, there is one thing that people are drawn to and will return to, and it's not about our knowledge and skills or our conversion and retention strategies–it is how attractive we are to them. The result of this is that they ascend to a higher version of themselves.

Attraction comes in many forms. How is it for your practice members? When your practice is attractive, your practice members want to come and see you. When you continue to stay attractive, they will stay, and refer their friends for a lifetime. This is the essence of the Attractive Practice Model.

While you may know that it's important to be attractive to bring people into your practice you might ask, "How long do I need to be attractive"? Pretty simple, I would say. As long as you want to have a vital, energetic, results-producing practice. Being perpetually attractive is the key for a lifetime of flourishing on all levels.

As with understanding the intricacies of most things, look to nature. For a flowering plant to get what it needs (pollination) it knows that it needs to be attractive to the bee. So, it produces what the bee needs – nectar. To attract the bee, the plant provides colour, scent and the sweet stuff, for as long as the need for pollination is there. As a result of this symbiotic relationship, the plant benefits, the bee benefits and the planet benefits. Without it our global food supply would be in dire straits.

We often forget this in our practice when our concern favours what *we* want and not what the practice member wants. This focus often leads to practices adopting the forceful short-term 'fix it now' approach which sees the practice and the practitioner caught up in the grind and minutiae of focusing on marketing, converting the new people, holding onto clients with strict retention methods and aggressive upselling.

The Attractive Practice Model is different. It resonates with the powerful vitalistic principle of playing the long-game. This brings the elevating, inspiring x-factor that continuously draws people to it, and does so naturally and without loss of integrity, force or false sincerity.

An example of this came up the other day when a coaching client contacted me with a question. He said, *"I'm just reviewing my CA contracts with the lawyers. They have recommended that I have a restraint of trade so that they can't go and work up the street or in a certain geographical area. This would stop another practice from poaching my CA".* My reply to him was, *"if your CA is poachable your practice isn't attractive enough".* I suggested that he remember the fact that people come and go in our lives/practices for a reason, a season or a lifetime. In my opinion our practice can be a vehicle by which people can ascend to their highest expression and, as long as we keep the game alive, green and growing we will continue to be attractive to them and them to us.

> *People will leave your practice when they run out of*
> *an attractive future.*

The Attractive Practice Model perpetually facilitates a compelling future for every person. There is no conversion, but there is lots of nurture. People feel safe and supported by predictable systems and processes. There is an attractive offering that is delivered with style.

Concerns around retention are not relevant when the practice is attractive. There is no upselling. The attractive practice naturally ascends people to their next level of development. They keep growing, and if they outgrow the practice, they leave with the practice's blessing and best wishes.

It's different, isn't it? Imagine that: a business based on inspiration, abundance and evolution, not on fear, lack and holding on?

We are about to embark on a transformative, deep dive into a new way of thinking about life in practice. You are about to discover the key to the Attractive Practice Model. The Quest Procedures For Lifetime Care is an easy-to-apply, brain-based model for practices and business that creates outstanding results as it infuses a vitalistic essence into operations. It is used extensively for chiropractic practices but can in fact be applied to any practice or business that respects an integrated view of life.

Be the observer as you embark on this journey. Notice your thinking as you go. You will see shifts – some subtle and some dramatic – as you digest, understand, and apply the Attractive Practice Model.

This system will challenge many of your preconceived beliefs about yourself and how your brain and practice works. It will enable you to harness the power of brain-based processes, so that you can adopt new ways of thinking and behaving which will give you more and better results in your personal and practice life.

The Attractive Practice Model is a method of creating enduring, lifelong relationships with the people who seek your care.

It's really quite a simple four-step formula.

1. *Be Attractive.*
2. *Systematise Attraction.*

3. *Have fun doing what you love.*
4. *Constantly reinvent yourself.*

Attraction breeds opportunity beyond all measure and is the antithesis of commonly touted lead-generation and retention methods of business growth. But it comes with a caveat. Attraction is not a set-and-forget thing. You must constantly pay attention to it at every level.

Welcome to the Attractive Practice Model where we journey together in this wonderfully integrated view of existence. May you, your team, your practice, and your practice members thrive.

My goal is to give you a step-by-step guide for you to grow your practice.

This book, along with the Quest Chiropractic Coaching program, has a nautical flavour to it. The metaphor of your practice being the vessel, you the skipper, your team the crew, and your practice members the passengers provides appropriate parallels. The Quest Chiropractic Coaching program caters to four levels: the students are safely in the Harbour, the new graduates in the Bay, the healthy, growing practices in the Ocean while the leveraged and profitable practices are at the Captain's Table.

The content here contains all the steps you need to take your practice to seven figures and beyond. It contains the same tried and tested strategies successfully used by untold numbers of chiropractors around the world. In these pages, and the online kit that accompanies them, are proven strategies, based on a uniquely insightful, brain-based model, that are simply transformative.

The Questers and I look forward to sailing on this transformative voyage with you.

Mark Postles D.C.

The Attractive Practice Model

You Are the Attractive Character

You and each of your team members are attractive characters in your own right.

Whether you are a new graduate, a seasoned practice owner or a CA your success depends on your attractiveness. You are a unique expression of life. Never to be repeated. This is your gift to yourself, your team, your practice members, and humanity. **You are the Attractive Character.**

A common misconception in practices is that we are there just to provide a service, technique or process, and that is what people come and pay for.

This is only a small part of the equation.

In my early days in practice, I used to think it was all about the adjustment. In this stage, I was at the top of my delivery game. I studied my technique and trained, trained, trained. I was able to perform some pretty awesome tricks and got great results for which people were very grateful. The trouble was that they would say, "Thank you so much, Mark", and then they were gone.

I barely noticed they had gone as I proceeded to perfect the next technical skill to master. I just got on with finding the next person who needed my help.

As I became a little more self-aware, I realised that while the clinical offering was important, I was really in the business of *relationships*. One hot August day in 1973 in a park in the USA state of Iowa, surrounded by a bunch of our chiropractic college friends, Jackie and I made a very simple wedding vow to each other. It was that we would be with each other as long as love lasted. To us, this promise has meant that we were (and still are) always in the process of doing attraction with each other. Some fifty years later, this promise is still front and centre.

I saw a similar story in my practice. People came to us because we were attractive to them, and they stayed because of what we built into that relationship over time.

It's a journey you go on with them for a reason, a season or maybe a lifetime. The attractiveness of your practice creates a magnetic pull that causes people to stay with you. To me, this is both thrilling and challenging. You can't just show up, give the bare minimum and expect a thriving practice to materialise in front of you. You must have a perpetually attractive offering and presence, reflecting the uniqueness of you.

> *You cannot be the attractive factor if you don't give yourself permission to think, live, move and act in the uniquely authentic way that is genetically accurate for you.*

Every colour has its place on a canvas. Every note has its place in a song. The lack of one is to the detriment of the whole. You have a responsibility to yourself and to the world to be who you are and to let your unique colour, note, frequency and vibration animate the world.

*The new graduates that have joined our practice over the years
have classically experienced a series of incremental pops which
have ascended them to new levels of service and productivity.
Each one of these pops involve an increased acceptance of self.
They are seldom driven by external criteria and almost always
a product of an internal realisation.*

You have something special to share with humanity. Some people may not be available to take part in that sharing, but that is about them. It is not a sign for you to dull yourself or become smaller. You have so much to share – an inner reserve of wisdom that only you can offer.

You will have doubts and questions about your worth. Acknowledge them and love who you are (warts and all). This allows your inner beauty to shine. As a Chiropractor you know many powerful truths, that you may take for granted, but are totally revolutionary to the average person. Allow the following ideas (and many more that will be prompted by the list) to be your guide to creating thoughts that you can form into daily affirmations, mantras, prayers or reflections.

Playtime

- I am unique.
- I have a powerful offering.
- Practice members come here to engage with something greater.
- I am that 'something greater' that people come to connect with.
- Every person I see has profound wisdom to share with me.
- I have incredible curiosity about every person I meet.
- I elevate humanity by serving more people.
- People love seeing me on a regular basis.
- I know that different people will connect with different practitioners and that's okay, because there is always enough, and we all have something to offer.

Summary

- You and each of your team members are attractive characters in your own right.
- Your success depends on your attractiveness.
- A common misconception is that you are in practice just to provide a service, technique, or process, and that is what people want.
- You have a responsibility to yourself and to the world to be who you are and to let your unique colour, note, frequency or vibration animate the world.

The Vitalistic Practice

Imagine a practice where *everyone* thrives. Your practice members rave about the care that they receive. Your team joyfully works as one, and you are smiling. Imagine the energy you feel when you get out of bed on a Monday and head into that practice, knowing that you will be surrounded by empowered people who are inspired towards the same vision and are vibrating together in a way that elevates the practice and all who engage with it.

How does that feel? What does it look like to you? Envision that.

In this practice, you can stick to your lane, do what you do best and make sure you have people who display their superpowers in the gaps. This is the Attractive Practice Model. You don't dread a day's work here. You don't get Mondayitis. You are more invigorated at the end of the day/shift than when you started. You are attracted to this practice as well, as it's everything you dreamed it would be.

Within a vitalistic model of life and of practice, there's an intelligence that will work automatically, provided there is no interference.

Chiropractors recognises that your brain is only the coordinating centre of your nervous system, dynamically interacting with its multiple intelligences or 'brains' throughout the body (eg your heart, your gut and your gonads). Likewise, there are many intelligences operating in your business. This style does not rely on top-down management. It is not afraid of robust conversations and differing points of view. As in the body, the Attractive Practice Model is a matrix of decentralised intelligence, with every part contributing its own attributes in an interdependent manner.

Over many years, I developed a model based on brain function which applies to every endeavour involving people and their behaviours, their relationships, and of course, their businesses or practices. It is called the in8model®.

The in8model®

The *in8model®* was built first on study and observations of personality preferences and the ways people interact with each-other and with life. This led me to the realisation that there is a neurological flow and an inherent completeness that occurs when we work through the four Quadrants of the brain and their associated organ 'brains', evident in every human being.

Given the plastic (or changeable) nature of your nerve system, and knowing that nerves that fire together wire together, it stands to reason that the encoding of your life experience creates the firing patterns of your nerve system which creates habituation which creates your identity. The Quadrant functions are a result of repetition over time and give you your preferences and behavioural traits.

Of course, a model is just a model. It does not form our entire reality. It does, however, help us understand and interact with our experience. There are certain ways in which human beings process data, some of which are optimum for their circumstances and others sub-optimal. The Attractive Practice Model takes this awareness of neurological preference and applies it in a practical way that allows each part of that living organism to thrive and cycle from strength to strength.

The *in8model®* is unconscious, yet, when brought to awareness, becomes obvious. This enables people to use the simple procedures to model behaviour useful for a given outcome, or to recognise behaviours in others that can be used for increased understanding, meaning, connection, and productivity in relationship, business, or team environments.

No two *in8model®* profiles are identical. Just as people are unique, so are the ways they perceive and process their world. This being the case, there are still patterns of preferences that will predispose people and practices to exhibit typical behaviours for the filters that they are using.

Let me give you an example.

Every one of us have people with whom we connect easily: our minds seem to meet instantaneously. We find connection, discussion, and agreement effortless. We also have those that are not so easy. There can be a struggle to connect, despite a genuine desire to do so.

When we cease thinking of personality traits as labels, static and immovable, and start thinking of them as recognisable preferences and remembering we have all parts inside, something interesting happens – we create connections where it was difficult before.

I recall this happening many times in my practice. I am like many chiropractors in the distribution of my in8model® preferences: I am good at Quadrants 1 and 3 (which you will become increasingly acquainted with over the course of the following chapters). People who are strong in these quadrants (which we will call Q1 and Q3 for ease throughout the rest of this book) are often big-picture thinkers, who care about people, connection and big ideas. We are not driven towards the details or numbers and facts. We want our people to be well, supported, cared-for, and feeling good. We were attracted to the big idea or philosophy of life and are animated by the ways in which it makes people's lives better.

This is what drives us to get out of bed in the morning and, with our hands and the tools at our literal fingertips, deliver life-altering force to remove the interference from the spines and nervous systems of our practice members. We come alive when we see *them* come alive. I connect easily with many types of people, but I recall one practice member with whom I didn't spark so easily.

His name was Frederick. He was nearly always wearing a tweed jacket with leather patches on the elbows. His glasses were on a chain around his neck and were set aside neatly when he approached the adjusting table. No matter how hard I tried to connect during the first couple of visits, the 'click' wasn't there. I started to wonder whether Frederick was a good fit for my practice.

Then came the 'aha' moment. From a place of understanding my preferred Quadrants, I was able to acknowledge his. He was an academic. He was driven to detail. He needed things to be correct and quantifiable. I was dealing with a strong Q2 preference. This was not a preferred Quadrant for me at that time. I recognised I had all parts inside of me, so I shifted gears in my relationship with him.

The next time I saw him on the schedule, I came armed with some chiropractic research. I made mention of a recent study that had come out. When I threw the findings into the conversation, he came alive. "Oh! How interesting! That means..." and off he went, conceptualizing what this research might mean for chiropractic and for the people who engage with it. There it was: the 'click' moment. In my care for Frederick, all I had to do was engage with his strong Q2 and he would conceptualise the rest. That was as easy as having a quick look at chiropractic research before he came in and offering up a little titbit that would make his day.

As well as being a very powerful insight into oneself and one's own drivers, the *in8model®* is useful in all areas of life. Loving relationships, business, sports and anywhere where two or more people gather, the skill of being able to understand and work with their unique neurological representation of their world is a powerful asset. If you can understand your own and another person's process, then you are able to expand your collective model of the world and facilitate more useful outcomes.

By completing the questionnaire and reading the *in8model®* book, you will get a good idea of where your preferences lie. This will explain how and why you live your life the way you do. The preferences of those people around you will also become evident as you explore the nature of the Quadrants.

The *in8model®* questionnaire is available online at our website, www. thein8model.com. When you have completed the online form, you will receive a personalised report so that you can consider your own behavioural preferences and how they serve you in differing circumstances. This questionnaire is a useful tool whether you are hiring, training, placing or even firing team members (including yourself).

The in8model® Quadrants

Let's take a quick tour of the *in8model®* so you can be familiar with the style that each Quadrant prefers.

Quadrant 1.

- Anything is possible!
- Dreamer - Entrepreneur
- Eternal Optimist
- "Why?"
- "Trust me, it'll work out"

Q1 is big picture, creative, gregarious, curious, playful, inspired, and thrives on change. It loves to inspire and enable you to live out your dreams and manifest your highest self. It is visionary, spirited, spontaneous, motivated, fast paced, expressive, and a big picture thinker.

Q1 associated body part is the heart which is in its happy place when filled with hope and joyful longing for the infinite possibilities conjured up by the right frontal cortex.

The Chiropractor with a dominant Q1 function (which is very common) has an entrepreneurial style. This is the initiator in a group, direct and supportive of others. This part can often be so caught up in the big picture that the finer details get lost in the excitement. Running late is common as this part gets absorbed in having fun with the practice members and easily loses track of time. Every book, seminar or workshop this practitioner goes to will generate a whole list of great ideas to be implemented on Monday morning before the team has even been able to implement the last ones.

This part can be frustrating to their team as they are so unpredictable, but at the same time they are so charming and lovely that the angst is soon forgotten!

Quadrant 2

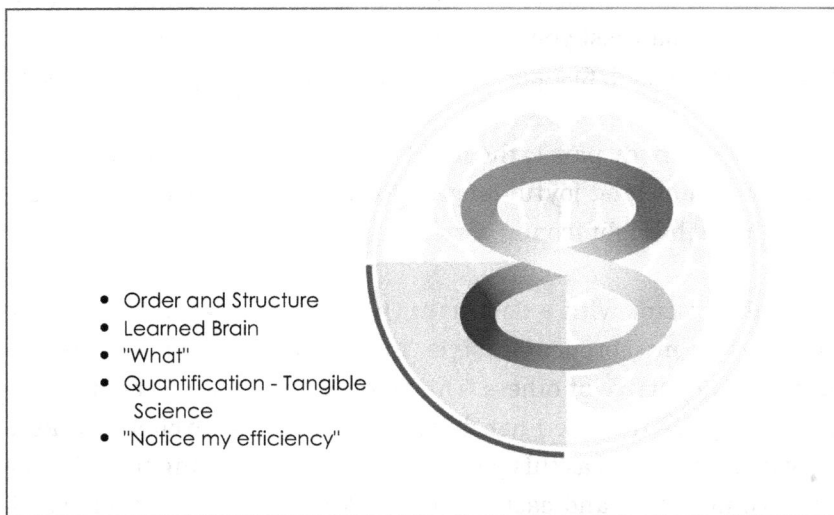

- Order and Structure
- Learned Brain
- "What"
- Quantification - Tangible Science
- "Notice my efficiency"

Q2 is the part that likes to be correct and precise. When you have information to process, you engage the left basilar area, and it is here that we research and sort out all the "fluff" that came through from Q1. The Q2 part asks the specific questions and dissects information into understandable detail. "What?" is the common expression of this area – it wants the content. This is the seat of order and structure – the home of the learned brain. It is the area that loves quantification and tangible, evidence-based science. Q2 computes slowly so most requests for change or improvement from the Q1 part are met with an initial "No". However, these ideas are later processed and responded to with a conditional reply.

Q2's theme is "notice my efficiency" and it will do whatever it takes to be correct and on time.

You will notice that the CA with a dominant Q2 function can get so focused on tasks that they miss connecting with the people in front of them. This part is super-efficient and neat, but can get overloaded with internal pressure and noise as they bear the load of everything that needs to be done. This part gets very stressed and often needs time to recover at the end of the day.

Quadrant 3

- Hardworking
- "How"
- Asks more than tell, listens more than talks
- Sensitive - connects with body
- Gut feeling

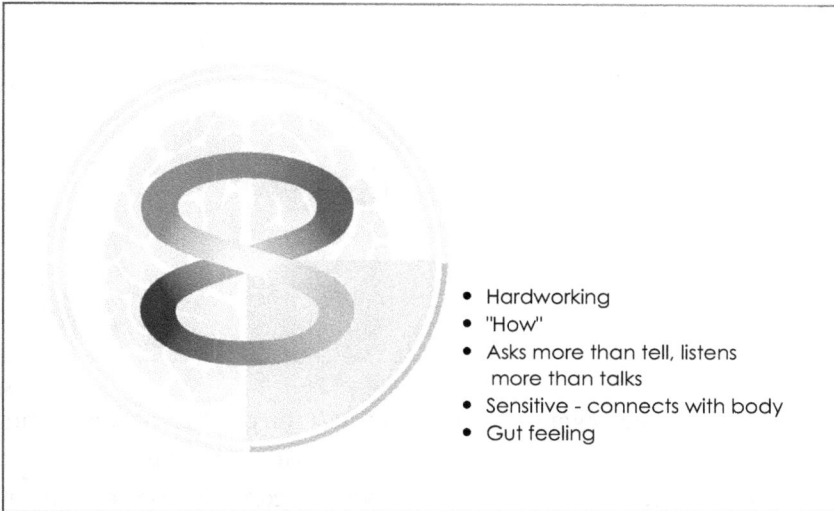

The Q3 part is amiable, adaptable, focused on people and connection, and is always seeking to serve through practical and person-focused means. It is thoughtful, tolerant, reliable, and relationship-oriented and it will always go out of its way to keep the peace, nurture the person, and bring the stabilising element to an interaction. This is the warm, practical, technique-focused, and relational element of the practitioner.

You may notice that the team member with a dominant Q3 part will be trying to please and make everyone happy. The Q3 tendency is to look after people and do for others that which they could do for themselves. This part is connected, solid, and hands on, while also often being indecisive and conflict avoidant. There is a tendency to take others' poor attitudes personally. There is a reluctance to confront or take control over practice members when it involves difficult conversations.

Quadrant 4:

- Universal Mind
- "What Else, What If"
- "Let's do it now"
- Politics
- Blunt
- Seizes Opportunities

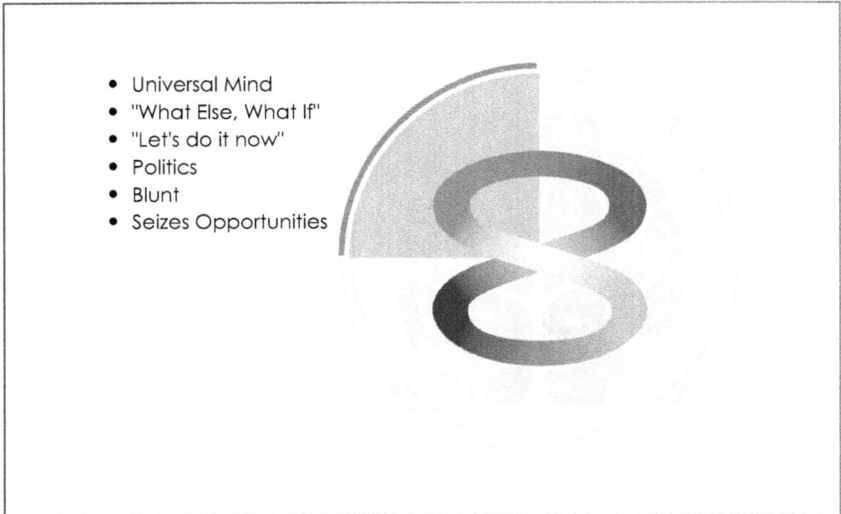

The Q4 part is your agent of change. It takes the product of Quadrants 1, 2 & 3 and develops it into greater possibilities. "What else?", "What if?" and "Where could we take this?" are the common expressions of this area – it wants the bottom line.

The Q4 preference is always ready to tell its opinion and does it with a high-volume, fast style of speech with challenging voice intonation. It tells more than asks and talks more than listens. True to its bottom-line nature, it is blunt and to the point. When it comes to moving on something, it is the part that seizes the opportunity and makes things happen – now.

It has been said by philosophers and quantum scientists alike that we are awash in a sea of information of which we are, for the most part, unaware. Q4 (along with its right brain partner, Q1) seems to make good use of this field of consciousness pulling in thoughts that are quite profound.

The Q4 dominant chiropractor gets sick of the team complaining and is just like, "Yeah, yeah, yeah, stop talking about it and just do it." This to-the-point Quadrant expression can feel intimidating to those who do a high Q3, and they will tend to not speak up and take a stand for fear of Q4 judgement and disapproval.

Your Practice and the in8model®

Whilst still a chiropractic student I attended a number of the legendary Parker seminars for practice success. Chiropractors would fly from all around the world to attend and many of the heaviest hitters in the profession would attend for the two hours at the commencement of each seminar, in which Dr James Parker, in his very dry and understated way, would outline the 'Parker Principles'. After this session many would fly home again without even attending the rest of the weekend. I could see why these legendary Chiropractors would do this – The Parker Principles were profound and provided us with a framework for our function as Chiropractors. For me, a total newbie to this profession, I was forever affected by the principle, *"Loving Service Is My First Technique."* It was what drove me to be fully engaged in my professional journey from checking and adjusting practice members, to coaching practitioners, to contributing on state and national associations and Chiropractic college boards over the decades.

It seems natural that so many heart-centred practitioners operate from strengths in these right-brained Quadrants. We engage with the philosophy and art of our offering and put it to work in ways which elevate people and free them up to be their best selves. We serve them and watch them come alive again. It's more than relieving pain and illness. It is empowerment. The inclusive, person-centred side of us thrives as people become animated and free under our care.

This is what makes practice so deeply satisfying.

Of course, there are Q2 and Q4 practitioners (although not nearly as common). The strong Q2 part is meticulous, evidence-based and thrives with policies, procedures, and research. The *science* of our discipline wakes us up and inspires this part.

The Q4-preferencing chiropractor is driven towards expansion through constant reinvention of themselves and their practice. Risk taking is encouraged and change is embraced in this part.

Here's the thing, though: for a practice to thrive, we need all four quadrants present and empowered.

> *The Attractive Practice Model is a system of four parts. It enables you to thrive by recognizing where the team's superpowers lie and adding others to fill the gaps.*

I was blessed in that my journey into chiropractic began at the same time as my journey into a lifetime partnership with my wife, Jackie. Her Quadrant preferences complemented mine – she is strong in the left-brained Q2/Q4. While I thrived on the right, she was able to bring order amongst chaos, structure to inspiration, and she always manages to remember to pay the bills on time. This "opposites attract" type partnership was fortuitous for us: it formed the basis of a lot of 'learning', which at the time was frustrating for both of us.

Over time, I've looked around at a lot of practices and seen something similar: those that thrive are the ones in which there is a strong Q2/Q4 complementing a strong Q1/Q3. This may, of course, come in many different shapes and combinations, but it's always the same: a practice that thrives is the one in which all Quadrants are given space to function.

Business Practice

Science   Philosophy
Profits   Art
Results   Relationships
Resources   Empowerment
Systems   Connection
Completion   Process

Sometimes it happens serendipitously. People stumble their way into a relationship or business partnership that enables them both to thrive. But there is a structure to it, so you can always do it by design.

It's so rewarding to see our coaching clients turn on the power in their teams as they get intentional about placing people for appropriate diversity. When this happens the energy and activity moves through the four Quadrants in that figure-of-eight process and the business constantly moves from strength-to-strength.

Yes, I said business. Not practice. If you are to devote your life to the creation of your practical magic, you need the business side to be sustainable. We have seen too many practitioners come to us for help with their practice after 30 or 40 years of hard work and they can't afford to retire or sometimes even take a holiday.

As practitioners, we must acknowledge that we are immersing ourselves in a heartfelt hobby and the hobby is part of a profitable business. When we see it from this perspective, we can be exquisite in the practice and astute in the business.

There are eight key strategies that apply to every practice regardless of philosophical persuasion. This model is not a system dreamed up by academics. It is a dynamic, living model, observed in all human interaction. From Plato and Aristotle through to the latest blockbuster movie or breakthroughs in behavioural science, you will find the same patterns reoccurring. In this model, you will be cycling through the levels at all time. Like spinning plates, you will be making sure that your business is always ascending to the next level as you are attending to the current relevant components.

Scoring Your Practice

The scoring is recorded on the dotted line drawn diagonally through the Quadrants. The centre of the 8 is the zero point and there are 15 increments out to the periphery through each quadrant. Typically, there may be one or two Quadrants that receive a higher score but sometimes several or even all Quadrants can be equal.

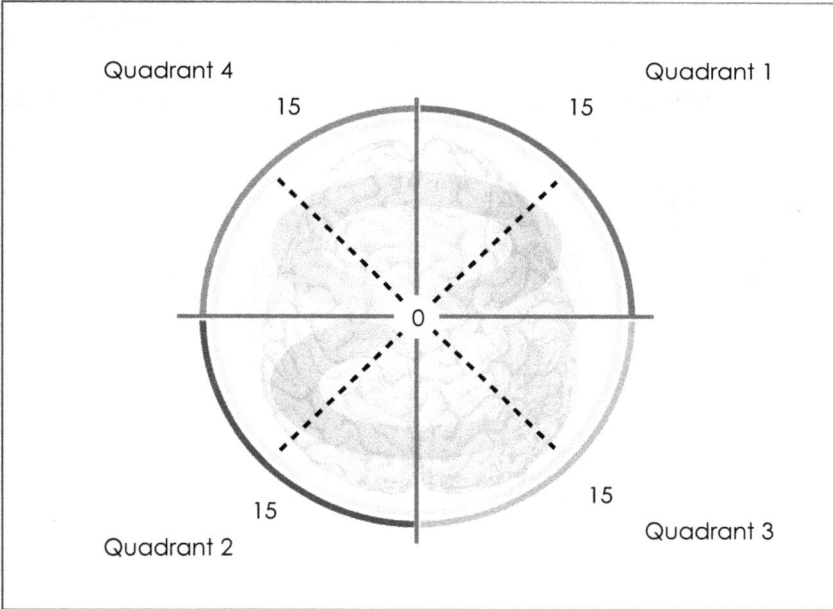

Quadrant 4 — 15
Quadrant 1 — 15
Quadrant 2 — 15
Quadrant 3 — 15
0

We all have all traits within us, and we use the ones that we prefer. This preference becomes our identity. We score in all Quadrants, so it's the relationship *between* the Quadrants that is the telling factor in terms of our thinking and therefore our behaviours and actions.

Go on. Do the test along with your team! Go to the in8model® free quiz and find out what your preferences are. If you want to dive deeper into the model itself, check out the *in8model®* book, and there are a number of courses that will help navigate various levels of engagement with the *in8model®*.

For the rest of this book, we will explore how the brain based *in8model®* provides a navigation map for your Attractive Practice Model.

- Do the free in8model®quiz at <u>www.thein8model.com</u> with your team.

Your Brain-Based Practice

The four key brain functions of human beings as outlined in the *in8model®* are essential elements of every practice and business. Why? Because they are rich, time-tested patterns echoed in nature and implementable in business. That is, once you understand the flow of an idea from intention to reinvention.

These four key brain functions look like this:

1. *ATTRACT is how you connect with people, establish your practice as credible, allow your vibration and message to resonate with them in a way that makes them eager to enter into agreement with you, start and continue care, and create a lifetime relationship with your practice.*

   The Result – FROM struggling to get new practice members TO an automated inflow of ideal new people.
2. *NURTURE is how you let people feel safe, secure and certain because you have a predictable, reliable and trusting relationship which sees them develop knowledge and wisdom.*

   The Result – FROM constantly putting out fires TO simple and effective systems and procedures.
3. *DELIVER is the excellent service, intimate and relevant communication that impacts them to the core, so they become a partner in your tribe of like-minded people.*

   The Result – FROM constantly changing tactics TO duplicatable clinical excellence.
4. *EXPAND is empowering practice members and your practice to higher levels of effectiveness. This frees everyone up for opportunities of greater contribution.*

   The Result – FROM the boss doing everything TO empowered leverage.

The Transformation

Before we embark, let's look at some of the things you can expect in the practice of this methodology.

Without the Attractive Factor	With the Attractive Factor
Your practice is predetermined by your market	Your practice is an expression of your choices
People's personality is set	People's personality is unlimited
People's behaviours are set	People have the ability to take on different behaviours
Try to make others work your way	You appreciate others' ways
Only feel comfortable with people like you	Feel comfortable with people unlike you
Your rules apply to everyone	Everyone has their own rules
There is a right way and a wrong way	There is always another way
We are under the control of a centralised authority	We are an inter-related part of a decentralised energy matrix
Pull back from challenging circumstances	Engage in challenging circumstances
Me/Us vs Him/Her/Them	'We' together in collaboration
We are divided by differences	We are united by our differences
It is important to be certain	It is useful to be questioning and curious
Answers lie in the content	Questions arise in the concept
Centralised hierarchical command	Decentralised matrix of responsibility

Avoid difficult questions	Engage in difficult questions
Normal/Average is the acceptable	Exquisite and unique is applauded
Mediocrity is acceptable	Excellence is saluted
Competition mode	Collaboration mode
Outside/In and Below/Up	Above/Down and Inside/Out
We are all separate	We are all inter-connected energy
Get new patients	Attract people
Convert patients	Nurture people
Retain patients	Be continually attractive
People visit you because they have to	People visit you because they love to

Summary

- The Attractive Practice Model is based on inspiration, evolution, and perpetual attraction, not on fear-based conversion and retention.
- You are the attractive character in the practice. You have a unique offering that people need.
- In the Attractive Practice Model, we recognise that we are in the business of relationships, not in the business of giving adjustments and being paid for that.
- The Attractive Practice Model rhythm is "Attract, Nurture, Deliver, Expand".
- It is based on the in8model® and uses a brain-based approach to life, practice and business.
- We have all parts within us. We are complete.
- Completeness comes from using all brain quadrants and represents the information flow from right brain to the left and back again as an idea is acted upon.

- There are no two in8model® profiles that are identical. Just as people are unique so are the ways that they perceive and process their world.
- The Quadrants are numbered 1-4 to give as neutral energy as possible.

I know that you will enjoy adding to the attractiveness of your practice, as will your team and practice members.

The Attractive Practice MODEL

Your business is either growing or it's dying – it cannot be maintained in a static state – no living system can.

The following 8 Strategies are key touchpoints in the growth from a practice to a sustainable business. In a supportive growth model, it evolves and constantly exceeds its previous best, going sequentially through the Quadrants as it builds upon itself. Under stress and protection, however, it devolves and shrinks to assume a lesser version of itself. This renders the practice less attractive to all stakeholders.

Within each Quadrant there are numerous strategies, and we will focus on two key strategies within each. The following diagram shows the layout of these strategies, which will form the core of the rest of this book.

The 8 Strategies Of The Attractive Practice Model

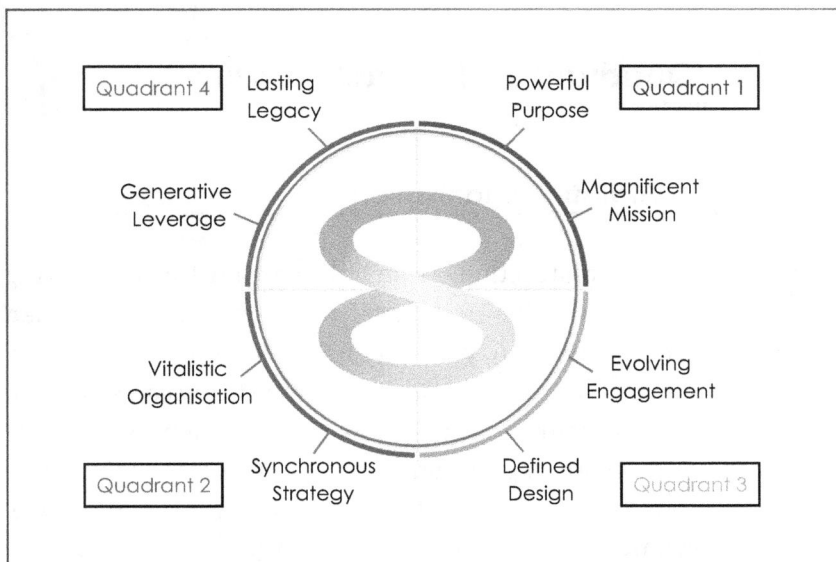

| Quadrant 4 | Lasting Legacy | Powerful Purpose | Quadrant 1 |

Generative Leverage — Magnificent Mission

Vitalistic Organisation — Evolving Engagement

| Quadrant 2 | Synchronous Strategy | Defined Design | Quadrant 3 |

43

Quadrant 1 – Always Attracting

Strategy 1 – Powerful Purpose

In Strategy 1, we look at the values and purpose that you hold as a practice. These will either support or sabotage you. Shifting any one of these to a more useful form will be transformative for you and your practice.

Strategy 2 – Magnificent Mission

In Strategy 2, we explore your mission. How clear are you on your direction and what you are here to accomplish? You are in a noisy world and being heard isn't about being louder. When you are clear on your mission you can quietly exude authority and whisper your wisdom at the right time and in the right place.

Quadrant 2 – Naturally Nurturing

Strategy 3 – Vitalistic Organisation

One of the greatest distractions from holding your line and letting your unique wisdom shine is internal pressure and noise. When you don't have organisation, you don't have certainty, and you and others around you don't feel nurtured. This one thing can send people running out of your practice. The key distinction here is that the organisation is an expression of the life force of the practice and not a scripted, top down, autocratic and hierarchical dictate. Vitalistic Organisation breathes life and vibrance into the attractive practice.

Strategy 4 – Synchronous Strategy

A simple success strategy is a must if you are to be attractive to your team and your practice members. Here you will fine-tune how to get people to rally around your strategy so that it sits well with them and resonates with your practice's values, purpose, mission, and goals.

Quadrant 3 – Delightful Delivery

Strategy 5 – Defined Design

The design of your clinical and educational offering must be seamlessly based on a congruent theme. Every stage of your practice design is choreographed to appear at the right time to add one more brushstroke to the masterpiece that it is.

Strategy 6 – Evolving Engagement

Focused engagement with your practice members allows you to have more meaningful connections. Your practice is in the people business above all else and they must experience your presence first and foremost.

Quadrant 4 – Energising Expansion

Strategy 7 – Generative Leverage

You leverage the activities of your practice so that others can duplicate your great work and take it further thereby generating the next iteration of your business. You let go of the day-to-day management and focus on your business from a governance level. Here you try and test the existing, generate and embrace the new and reinvent your practice to scale to the next level.

Strategy 8 – Lasting Legacy

Through empowering others to excel at their next level you generate a sustainable practice which runs on its own momentum. Your practice becomes an institution, constantly ascending to higher levels of impact and contribution. It oozes abundance and prosperity without your direct involvement.

Quadrant 1: Always Attracting

The 8 Strategies Of The Attractive *Practice Model*

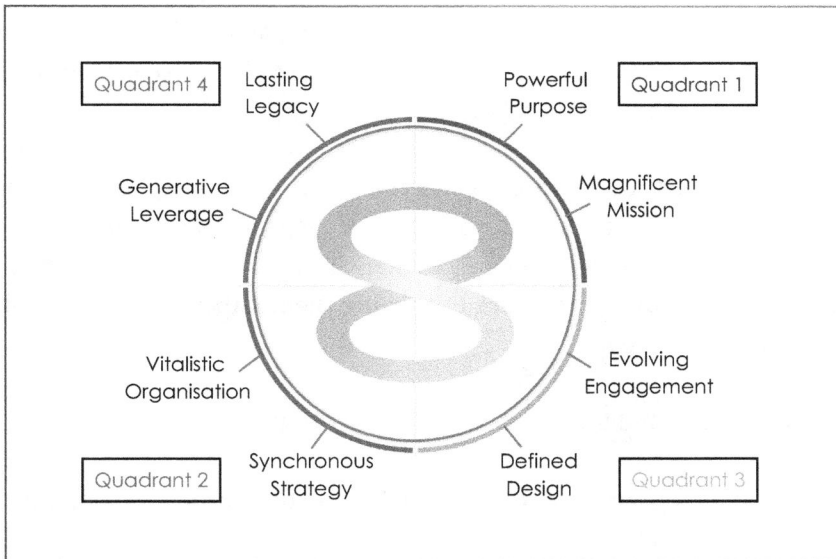

Phil had tried everything before. He came to us looking for help as the last resort. He had tried all the tricks and tactics on attraction, conversion and retention learned from books, seminars, coaches and gurus. He was frustrated with his revolving-door practice and was convinced that his patients were "dumb/stupid/ignorant" and a bunch of other descriptors. He also knew that his skills were, as he put it, "pearls in front of swine". New people would show up for the

first few visits and then they were up and off, never to be seen again (or not until their next 'problem').

He knew that he was not giving the best care that he could. He was aware that his impact on people's relationships, confidence, sleep, physical and mental health, wealth, community contribution and the like were sub-optimal.

In short, he and his practice were unattractive in so many ways.

We began the systematic process of bringing the WOW factor of attraction into every aspect of the practice. He realised that he had been focussed on the things that mattered to him (brain, spine, nervous system, subluxation, etc.) rather than the things that mattered to them. With coaching and the appropriate systems, he steadily made the changes towards the powerful state of Always Attracting. As they say, the rest is history. The practice got legs of its own. Team morale escalated, the culture flourished, and the practice members stayed, paid and referred like crazy.

The lost opportunity cost of people not coming into your practice for care when you are ready and able to serve them is massive on so many fronts. You have invested hugely in many areas to be able to help people. It is not okay that you are not seeing the numbers of people that you could provide for.

This costs you and humanity in numerous ways.

In this chapter, we look at the initial attraction of people into your world.

To provide results for yourself and others, you must have people to attend to. To have these people, you can either go out and drag them in with trickery, force and coercion, or you can draw them in by being attractive and offering them what they desire in a way that pleases them on an ongoing basis.

In times gone by, it was sufficient just to trawl the malls to acquire a supply of new patients. Now, in our information-heavy world, we realise that often it takes much more than one exposure for a person to move towards your practice. A person must know us, like us and trust us before they make the move to join us. If you think about the formula for filling your practice it would look like this:

**ATTRACTIVENESS x NUMBER OF TOUCH POINTS =
A GROWING PRACTICE**

It's quite simple, really. The degree to which you and your practice are attractive to people multiplied by the number of times people are exposed to that attractiveness results in practice growth.

This section is focused on the part of the business brain that we refer to as 'Attract'. It is the Q1 part of the in8model®. Now, it doesn't mean that attraction is just a Q1 function (far from it), but it is the driver for an attractive person and an attractive practice, and that attractiveness gets infused in all aspects of your practice through specific strategies.

In this section, we will cover two key strategies that are essential to your attraction. They are a Powerful Purpose and a Magnificent Mission. But before we do that, we need to look at four major influencers of all relationships and therefore all strategies. These are Hope, Trust, Skills and Narrative.

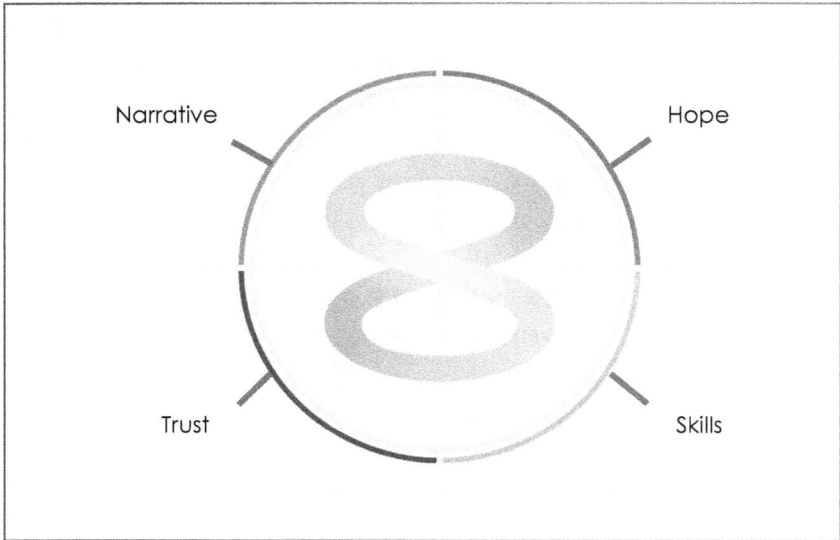

Q1 – Hope

I am sure that hardly a day goes by in your practice without a practice member thanking you for restoring their hope in themselves and their body's incredible ability to function at a higher level.

One of your greatest instruments of helping and healing is hope. If we take hope away from a practice member, we are negatively affecting their life force and directing them on a devolving pathway.

Good evidence for hope abounds: research shows that hope helps support mental strength and happiness, optimism, positivity and emotional control. It improves general health, reduces stress, reduces joint pain, improves respiration, reduces anxiety, improves social relationships, motivates positive action, leads to real-life success, strengthens the immune system, broadens and builds the mind, leads to courage, confidence, and self-efficacy, better grades and high-quality friendships.

Napoleon Bonaparte is quoted as saying, "A leader is a dealer in hope." You, as a chiropractor, must make sure that you are a dealer in hope. Every interaction with your practice members is an opportunity to instil hope in them. It is not about false hope either. It is about looking for anything that is right and focussing on that whilst linking it to the person's situation.

The great Scottish reformist and author, Samuel Smiles, once stated, "Hope is the companion of power, and mother of success; for who so hopes strongly has within him the gift of miracles."

Hope is a move away from the past and the present into the future. The more clearly you can paint the picture of the future for your practice members the more they will be neurologically drawn to that compelling vision.

Summary

- Hope is a powerful tool for healing.
- Hope has many benefits, including supporting mental strength and happiness, reducing stress, and improving overall health.
- As a chiropractor, it is important to instil hope in people during every interaction.
- Hope is about focusing on what is right and linking it to the person's situation.
- The more clearly a chiropractor can paint a picture of a better future for people the more they will be drawn to that vision and motivated to work towards it.

Q2 – Trust

The Trust Formula

There are four key 'deposit' mechanisms into the 'bank account' of trust. These reflect the four brain Quadrants of the *in8model®*. These must all be in place. If only one of these factors is absent or minimal, it sabotages every deposit you try to make into the trust account.

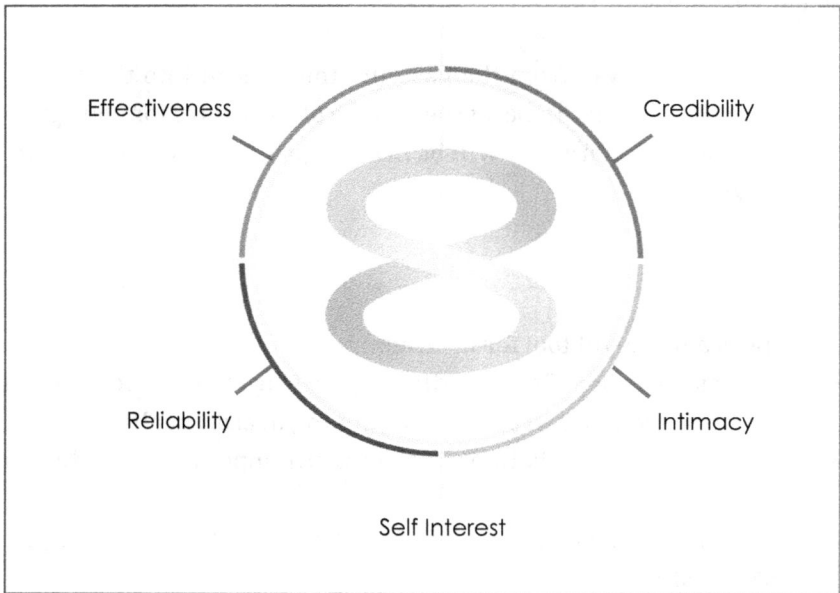

Effectiveness   Credibility

Reliability   Intimacy

Self Interest

Credibility – You must be a credible source of sustenance when it comes to hope and health for practice members. The more your practice is a haven for their needs, the more people will be attracted to you.

Reliability – Reliability is an essential part of trust. People must be able to count on you. Practice members must know that you and your team will show up and do things in a certain way, and they will get the experience they desire.

Intimacy – As professionals, we are so privileged to work with people up close and personal. The more you connect and engage with your people the more they feel that you are a part of their 'inner circle'. This is sacred territory.

Effectiveness – You can ace it in attracting, nurturing, and delivering, but if the results aren't evident, then trust is eroded. Having evidence of results is critical in the trust-building process. Results come in many forms, defined by both parties. Results may go far beyond the presenting complaint, which, incidentally, may never resolve, but the results for that person, in many other dimensions, may be profound. This produces enthusiasm and a desire to spread the word.

Self-Interest – The degree to which you are concerned about yourself and your interests is the degree to which you will create withdrawals from the bank account of trust. People sense self-interest coming a mile away. They've been attuned to it through disingenuous sales attempts all their lives. They know when they are being prospected or upsold and when they receive that message, they also receive the message that you are not on their team.

A significant element of self-interest is the fear of being rejected or disliked and hence not recommending the care that is necessary. Alternatively, when someone encounters a practitioner who is completely *in*, boots and all, who is driven and inspired by a passion to serve, and who sees the very best in their practice members, the effect is entirely different.

Building Trust

Building trust starts with an analysis of where you are now. What percentage of your practice members are staying and referring for a lifetime? Your practice statistics of people's ascension (Total Visits divided by New People as a trailing average over at least six months), lifetime value (Total Income divided by New People over at least three years if possible), the Average Fee and Referral Sources show this. If you don't have these figures, then it is prudent for you to invest the time and effort in getting them, because you cannot manage what you cannot measure.

Summary

- Trust is the currency being traded in a practitioner-practice member relationship.
- Trust is built by setting clear outcomes and agreements.
- When trust is broken, loyalty is lost and the practice member disappears from the practice.
- Practitioners often focus on attracting new people, but neglect to maintain trust with current ones.
- A fragmented approach to practice strategy does not build trust.
- The in8model® offers a structure based on brain science to build trust and predictability.

Q3 – Skills

Your 90 year old grandmother may have great love and hope for you. You may trust her as an amazing woman BUT if she doesn't have chiropractic skills it would probably not be useful to have her adjust you. Skills are critical to your success.

Generating hope and trust plus having the skills and techniques that consistently produce incredible results will create exponential growth.

We know that structure affects function, and we also know that human beings are biped and have an optimal relationship to gravitational forces. As chiropractors our interest is in optimal function and optimal (low energy) adaptation to gravitational forces. Regardless of your technique, ensure that you check your practice members relative to their load bearing before a specific adjustment and then run the same checks after the adjustment. This pre/post system demonstrates to you, the practitioner, and to the practice member, the efficacy of the adjustment and provides a comparison point for their journey.

Malcolm Gladwell in his book 'Outliers', states that "10,000 hours of practice is the magic number of greatness." While there are exceptions to this statement, it is worth bearing in mind as you undertake your professional commitment to lifelong learning.

The point here is that, to the degree that you are exquisite and effective with your skills, you will complement the hope and the trust that people have in you.

Summary

- Having the necessary skills and techniques is critical for success in chiropractic practice.
- Generating hope and trust, along with consistent results, leads to exponential growth.
- Effectiveness in skills will complement the hope and trust that practice members have in the practitioner and attract more like-minded people.

Q4 – Narrative

Every profession has its philosophy, science and art. However, it is not a profession until it professes. Your philosophy, science and art must have a way of expanding. This is through the narrative that you create.

The narrative is the political expression of the former three points (the *in8model*® Q4). It is this point that constantly wants to build and develop what currently exists to be better and more beneficial. It wants more people to know about it and distribute it to more people.

The Q4 part sees that everything can be better; it stands up and professes, with its time, money and voice.

However, as with any powerful force the power of narrative must be used with due respect for outcomes and the sensitivities of the recipients. Unfortunately some chiropractors get the 'cart before the horse' and try to force their chiropractic narrative on others before the person is ready to take it on board. A defensive response results, despite the hope, trust and skills boxes being ticked.

Having the patience and sense of timing to layer the chiropractic narrative over (in some cases, a long) time creates the opportunity for practice members to scale to utilising your service at higher levels. You never know, some of them may end up as chiropractors!

You are here to serve with your heart (Hope), head (Trust), hands (Skills), and voice (Narrative) and, as long as you do it with selfless focus, you will be an attractive character creating an attractive practice which results in an attractive business.

Summary

- The narrative is the political expression of a person's, group's or profession's philosophy, science, and art.
- A profession is defined through its narrative.
- It is important to use the power of narrative with respect for recipients and their sensitivities.
- Patience and timing are important when layering the narrative, to allow practice members to fully utilise your services.

Management by agreement

Obviously, every person who seeks your care is coming from a different place (culture, education, world view, etc.), and will be desiring their own unique outcomes. It's your job to connect with them and their wishes, hopes and dreams, and create a mutual agreement about the direction of your relationship.

In the Quest model every stage of your relationships with others must be framed with an agreement. These form a basis for trust to be created. Completing on your agreements allows trust to build. This is the process that we refer to as Management by Agreement. QPFLTC ensures that every step of the journey in your practice is management by agreement.

Playtime

- Make sure that you have agreement frames in place for EVERY stage of your practice member's journey.

Strategy 1: Powerful Purpose

The 8 Strategies Of The Attractive Practice Model

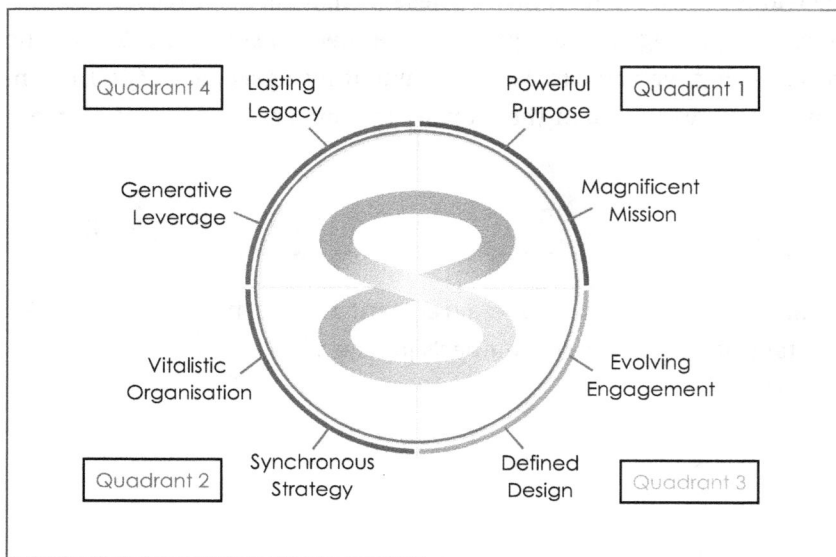

Quadrant 4	Lasting Legacy		Powerful Purpose	Quadrant 1
	Generative Leverage		Magnificent Mission	
	Vitalistic Organisation		Evolving Engagement	
Quadrant 2	Synchronous Strategy		Defined Design	Quadrant 3

Your purpose for doing everything is reflected in the 'thing' you are doing right now. Your practice is a reflection of your collective purpose, so let's take a few minutes to assess the structure of purpose and consider how we can discover and amplify your purpose.

The great Socratic imperative, "Know Thyself" tells us that the first step is self-awareness. Some would say Powerful Purpose is a 'fluffy' subject. However, every function has a structure, and you may find the following model useful.

Powerful Purpose

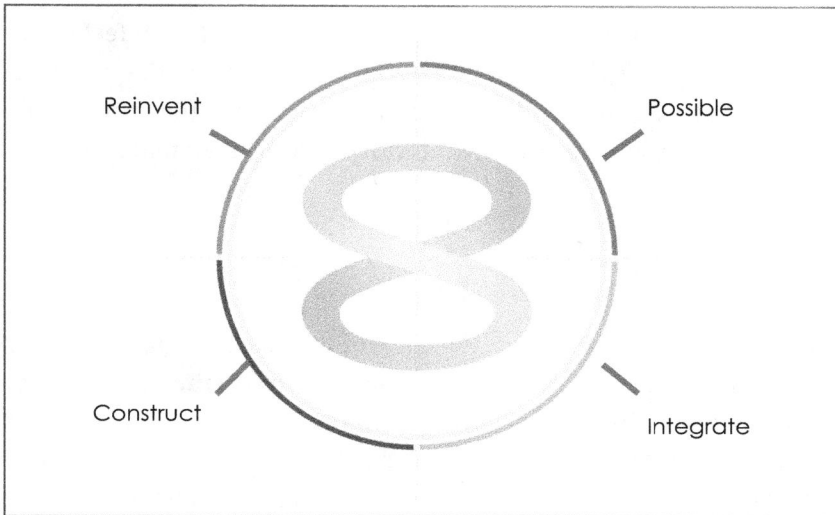

As an overview, consider the neurological structure of your purpose:

Q1 – Possible

Step 1. – You look into the future and scan the infinite **possibilities** that are before and beyond you. You ask why and why not. You romance the highest levels of your reason for being and your heart pounds with excitement.

Q2 – Construct

Step 2. – The vision is then passed to Q2 which is made up of your memories of past experiences, values and beliefs. Q2 searches for safety and probability. These 'rules' are blocks or accelerators of Q1's enthusiasm. From this consideration a **construct** of reality is created that gives the go-ahead to the Q3 part.

Q3 – Integrate

Step 3. – When given a strategy, the Q3 part will get the gut feel of this well-formed purpose, and craft plans for its implementation and **integration**. Naturally driven towards making a vision of the future manifest, the Q3 part will dutifully work with purpose and intent towards it.

Q4 – Reinvent

Step 4. – Never satisfied with the current purpose, the Q4 part is continually looking to **reinvent** and improve it. New distinctions and left-field ideas will flow from the Q4. This innovation will disrupt and annoy the 'steady as she goes' Q3 and 2 parts whilst the Q1 part will get all excited about the next iteration of the practice purpose and the possibilities within – and so goes the cycle of evolving one's purpose.

Values Determine Outcomes

Ask yourself who you are, and you will find yourself coming up with words that describe certain behaviours or labels. They may be words like: creative, thoughtful, precise, punctual, kind, etc. These are your values. They are positive or negative charges that you have applied to something. The sum total of your values produces your identity. It is worth noting that it is not necessarily *you*, but rather the lens through which you see life.

The process of how you accomplish anything in life may be seen as a complex series of specific neurological steps. The combination of these steps produces certain behaviours, much like the specific combinations of black lines on the barcode of a supermarket product label brings up different product information from a database. Just one line being a little thicker or thinner than another changes the whole meaning of that bar code.

The combination of behaviours, their outcomes, and the meanings you ascribe to them become your life's journey. The choices you make determine your outcomes. Will you be an unconscious passenger? Will you stay within the confines that others have built for you, like the boundaries that make up a harbour? Or will you gain mastery over the grey matter and proceed to the open ocean where new exploration can be made?

Getting results in life is the product of specific neurological steps being taken in an appropriate order, consistent with the outcome. Things don't just happen randomly. The clothes we wear, the food we eat, the houses we live in, the cars we drive; all are products of these neurological steps. There is a cause-and-effect relationship involved. This applies as much to you and your personal life as it does to your attractive practice.

The way humans process their world is laden with uniqueness, and yet, within that spectrum of individuality there seems to be two opposing paradigms:

- There is the **mechanistic paradigm,** which holds that all matter and the resulting life forms are simply collections of atoms (in this paradigm said to be the smallest components of matter), in different forms. This viewpoint suggests that people are all the same, that we are at the mercy of our world and are essentially victims of circumstance. It supposes that, given the opportunity, people will make the wrong choices and therefore need to be controlled and managed to do the right thing. The method of this **outside/in** approach tends to treat people as a herd and attempts to provide a one-size-fits-all solution to their problems. This paradigm is evident in many areas of education, politics, and medicine, to name a few, and is characterised by high levels of control and management.
- The other viewpoint, commonly known as the **vitalistic paradigm,** recognises that all we know as 'real' is in fact energy. People

are unique individual expressions of this energy. This viewpoint suggests that people are *causing* their world rather than being *effected* by their world and that, given a suitable environment, they will make the most appropriate choices. The method of this **inside/out** approach is to treat people as individuals, without labels.

Every thought, word, or deed that we entertain in ourselves or in our practice reflects one or the other of these critical paradigms.

Core Values

Your practice's moral reference point is expressed in and through your core values.

Core values are an essential part of every healthy and vital organisation. They point towards the team's moral reference point and sense of true north. Here, in these values, is the team's sense of identity, operations and culture.

Your core values create the uniqueness of your practice. They can be joined with other values to yield an operational statement that defines a certain part of your practice and will guide it as it develops into a business.

They could be like this:

- Fun filled, transformational shifts
- Scintillating WOW-factor
- Inspiration and connection
- Thriving people
- Lovingly supportive and challenging
- Vitalistic perspective on life

- Excellence in everything
- Oozing abundance
- Total authenticity
- Consistent and predictable results

The collective core values are the non-negotiables of your practice. They determine the culture, the tone, and the filter through which all other actions of the business are founded. What are your core values? What are your practice's core values? Just because we all came up through chiropractic school, and all chose to serve humanity this way, doesn't mean our values are identical. Doing the work (we call it play) to discover, clarify and express them is important.

Playtime

- Identify your personal values.
- Identify your practice's core values.
- Revisit them and tweak them on a regular basis.
- Give us a call at Quest if you want help in this critical area.

Summary

- The first step in self-awareness is the Socratic imperative, "Know Thyself".
- The Powerful Purpose model includes:
  - Q1, romancing the highest levels of reason for being,
  - Q2, searching for safety and probability,
  - Q3, crafting plans for implementation and integration, and
  - Q4, constantly looking to improve and tweak the purpose.
- Values determine beliefs, behaviours, actions and outcomes, and ultimately produce identity.
- The neurological steps that you apply in your personal life also apply to your professional life.

Your Affirmational Statement of Purpose

We've talked about trust, hope and inspirational core values. Now let's look at how they play out in your life and practice. For your practice to be attractive, you and your team must be attractive.

This happens completely by design. This is where the glorious and transformative work of the Attractive Practice Model journey begins – this is your collective purpose, your cultural 'true north'.

At Quest, we regularly see our clients' practices taking major leaps in growth immediately after they discover, refine, and own their purpose.

Now, before we go any further let's get the terminology sorted. The terms purpose, outcomes, goals, and mission are often used interchangeably, and yet they serve very different functions in life and business. Let's look at a quick definition and example.

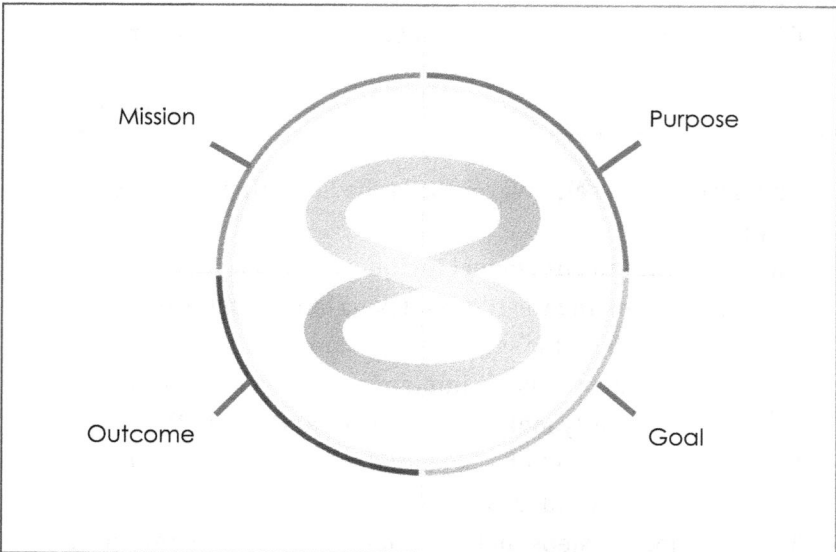

Mission

Purpose

Outcome

Goal

Q1 – Purpose

This is your big reason for being, having and doing. Everything is governed by your purpose. Let's think of this as the song in your heart. This occurs wherever you are and wherever you go. Your purpose reflects in what you do and how you do it.

Q2 – Outcome

Your purpose often guides you through deciding on an outcome. The outcome is the direction you are going. For example, "to be a great skilled (name your technique) practitioner." This function creates the strategy and the plan going forward for the next step.

Q3 – Goal

The next step are your goals, measurable and quantifiable. It may be numbers of new people, people served, etc., or it may be expertise in a given area. Goals are attainable and specific, unlike purpose and outcomes.

Q4 – Mission

The mission is the actions taken to achieve the goal. For example, you may be on a mission to make your offering an essential component of everybody's healthy lifestyle.

Now, it's one thing to have discovered and romanced your purpose, but it's another to integrate it into your neurology. This is where the Affirmational Statement of Purpose comes in.

We regularly see practices rapidly expand when they establish their Affirmational Statement Of Purpose.

> *Tanya comes to mind in this context. She had struggled with low New People numbers, low PVA and high staff turnover. In frustration, she reached out to us for help. After doing an audit on her practice, we saw that she had pretty good procedures and was delivering a competent service, but there were incongruencies between what she and her team said their intent was and what they were actually doing. The first thing we did with Tanya was to get her values reflected in a congruent Statement of Purpose. It was like a light was switched on. Within a few weeks the practice was overrun with new people, the compliance went way up, the team were excited about their roles in the practice, and of course, the numbers and income shot up.*

Your affirmational Statement Of Purpose is your tribal event that stirs the collective values of the team and releases the energy from within. This brings the big possibilities of the future into the present moment and inspires you and your team to enact it now.

A great purpose statement is something that is birthed, not just written. You can't smash it out in an hour. It's not about blowing the cobwebs off some old thing you wrote back at a seminar years ago. For this exercise, you go deep. You look into the field of possibilities that you see in your future. You then set it in the present, phrasing it in a way that you, your team, and your practice members can connect with. In doing so, you are building a magnet that will attract people to the cause to which you are devoted and the future you envision.

At Quest, we coach people through this seminal piece of work using the four rules and the four essential topics of the Statement of Purpose. Sometimes you need a guiding hand to take you past the mental blocks that prevent you from discovering the great and expansive purpose that is yours. It's far too easy to think, "It's just little 'ole me in this little 'ole town delivering little 'ole services."

But that's not it at all. You, in your amazing town, delivering your incredible services to your intelligent practice members have an immense global impact. What if the next person you see was to become the next world leader or a Nobel Prize winner or the scientist behind a world-changing breakthrough? The cost of not being on point with your purpose is immense.

Remember that the Statement of Purpose is an internal instrument. It is a tribal chant. It is not for the public to see, so don't hold back on its expression. You can recite it at any time, but I suggest that you and your team do it at the completion of your team meetings. It should be a 'goosebump' experience where even newcomers to the team feel a kinaesthetic hit when they hear it. I suggest that you choreograph it to include movement, to further express the words you are using.

I'm deliberately not telling you the words of ours or any of our clients' practices' purpose statements. You're going to have to invent your own. But I can tell you this: it sets the tone for the shift to follow. It focuses each one of us on our 'true north'.

The Kinaesthetic Anchor

Your Affirmational Statement of Purpose will be turbocharged when you integrate it into your collective physiology. Consider the All Blacks, the legendary rugby world-beaters. One of this team's key points of power is the anchoring of the culture that is derived from the Haka that is performed at the beginning of a match. This tribal challenge strikes trepidation into the hearts of the opposition, giving obvious advantage to the All Blacks.

One thing is for sure. Anchoring your purpose, aspirations, and values at the end of every team meeting will put your practice on steroids.

Playtime

- Set a target date to have your practice's Affirmational Statement of Purpose created.
- Make sure that you have your kinaesthetic anchor on full bore.

Summary

- The Attractive Practice Model journey begins with discovering, refining and owning the collective purpose.
- Purpose is the reason for being, having, and doing everything.
- Outcomes are the direction you are going.
- Goals are measurable and quantifiable.
- Mission is to achieve a certain event or collection of goals.
- Establishing an Affirmational Statement of Purpose is important to integrate the purpose into the neurology of you and your team.

Beliefs

The sum total of your limiting and empowering beliefs determines your practice outcomes.

Purpose and philosophy determine our beliefs. It is important to do beliefs that serve you. It's fair to say that your beliefs right now are a collection of perceptions that you have taken on board and made into stories about how life is. They are there to keep you safe, psychologically and physically, as you make your way through the world. Some of these beliefs may be useful whilst others may not, and yet you may have done many of them for a long time without question.

The nice thing about beliefs is that they can change quite quickly in the light of new information or experience, whereas values are much more entrenched and take much more energy and time to shift.

Ask yourself the following questions and notice where you have empowering beliefs and where you have limiting beliefs.

- What do you believe about you? (Your aptitude as a professional, a technician, a manager, an owner, etc.)
- What do you believe about your profession? (Are you proud, ashamed, embarrassed, etc?)
- What do you believe about your practice members? (Do/don't they want to invest in themselves, can/can't they afford care, do/don't they want to refer friends to you, etc?)
- What do you believe about your team? (Are they excited, bored, committed to working with you? Are they capable, trustworthy, honest, etc?)
- What do you believe about your associates? (Are they contributing, growing, trustworthy, talented, etc?)
- And for each of these things, why?

Now that they're written, can you see the quality of your beliefs? Can you see the limiting and the empowering beliefs?

Remember that all of your practice members have an array of values, beliefs and purposes. There are no two people with the same hierarchy. The majority of your practice life is about weeding out un-useful beliefs in yourself, your team and your practice members. It is the practices that have useful and powerful purpose, congruent beliefs and behaviours that are attractive. In this state, they flourish.

Playtime

- Make a list of your empowering and limiting beliefs about yourself and your practice.

Summary

- The success of your practice is determined by the sum of your limiting and empowering beliefs.
- It is important to examine your beliefs in the context of purpose and philosophy.
- Your beliefs are a collection of perceptions and stories about how life is.
- Beliefs exist to keep you safe.
- Some beliefs may be useful while others may not.
- Beliefs may have been held for a long time without question.
- It is important to identify limiting and empowering beliefs in yourself, your team, and your practice members.
- Weed out un-useful beliefs in order for your practice to flourish.

Outcomes

When we first worked with Greg, he was a new graduate working in the UK as an associate. He went to a heavily mechanistic college and as a result, was inculcated in left brain oriented information and the data. He stumbled his way around technique, but found it a challenge, as he couldn't easily quantify it. There were no set doses, per se, and it was something he found difficult to wrap his head around.

Here was an intelligent guy who had been conditioned, via university, towards a very limited model of health care, using subjective outcomes, mainly pain. He was questioning the validity of a system that treated a part that is in pain until it's out of pain. He was wondering whether this limited model was what he wanted to do for his professional journey.

Greg began coaching with us at Quest. It has ended up being a rewarding partnership lasting more than fifteen years (so far). My outcomes for Greg were huge. I could see the potential in him, and I saw it as my role to awaken him to his greatness in whatever way I could.

He worked on encompassing the vision and possibilities that exist within chiropractic, and how magnificent and powerful that is. Over the years, he has assimilated the beautiful combination of right and left brain integration, one that sees his elegant handling of data and information, along with his advanced skills in philosophy and technique.

He has now developed the skill of reinventing himself over and over again: from an associate, to having his own practice, to having one associate and now an increasing number of associates. He has now written a book, become a world leader in his technique, travelled the world inspiring and informing chiropractic groups, becoming a Quest coach and is now spearheading a new private chiropractic college in South Africa.

You have the power to create outcomes way beyond that which you deem possible, both for yourself and others. First, get crystal clear on your purpose, mission and outcomes. Then your personal journey, your practice, your team, and your practice members' journeys will attract the people, situations, places, things, money (add whatever you wish), in abundance.

Remember, that outcomes are a reference point. The outcome is a defined direction and you may vary from it along the way. Consider the analogy of taking a journey and deciding that you are heading west. You may have goals along the way (which may be slightly off the outcome of 'west'), but you regather yourself and return to west when appropriate.

You must ensure that your outcomes for your practice members are accurately communicated and agreed upon by both parties. Attractive practices are managed by outcome agreements. These agreements are the foundation of your relationships.

Outcomes with your practice members revolve around you doing what you say you are going to do, and ensuring they do likewise. This is necessary for the integrity of the journey. Make sure that you take 'snapshots' of moments in time. These are known as Progressive Exams. Compare them against previous exams to see the progress. These evidence procedures can be both subjective and objective. They are not the end goal; they are simply evidence that the person is progressing in the direction of their outcome.

As a person ascends, you raise the bar. Initially, it may be the resolution of the problem that brought them to you, but as they ascend in their journey, additional expansions and clarifications of their outcomes are agreed upon. This is the essence of growth. (We will delve into these details when we embark upon Strategy 5 – Defined Design).

Playtime

- What are your personal outcomes?
  - Spiritually
  - Mentally
  - Physically
  - Family
  - Socially
  - Professional
  - Business
  - Financial
- What are your outcomes for your practice members?
  - Their care
  - Their health
  - Their life
  - Their understanding of chiropractic

Summary

- You have the power to create outcomes that are beyond what you believe is possible for yourself and others.
- Be crystal clear on your purpose, mission, and desired outcomes.
- Attractive practices are managed through outcome agreements, which are the foundation of relationships.
- To track progress, it's important to take 'snapshots' of moments in time through progressive exams.
- Regularly review and adjust outcomes as growth occurs.

Strategy 2: Magnificent Mission

The 8 Strategies Of The Attractive Practice Model

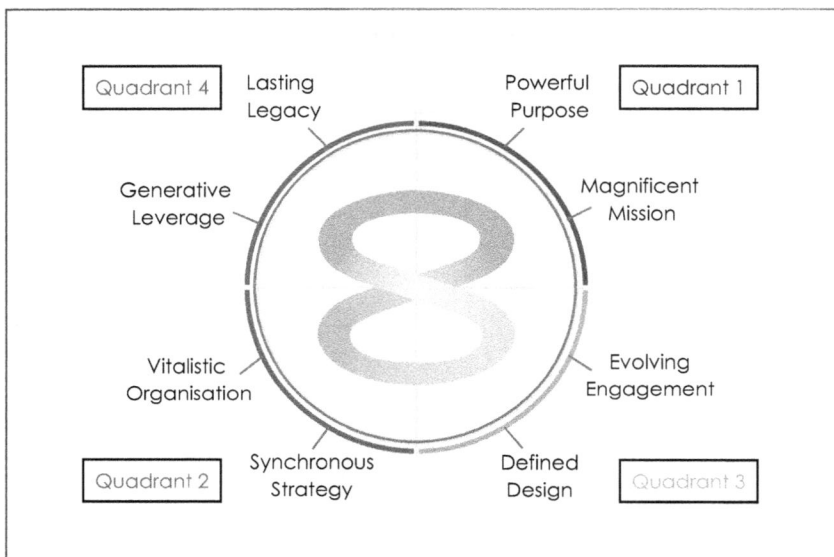

Quadrant 4	Lasting Legacy		Powerful Purpose	Quadrant 1

Generative Leverage

Magnificent Mission

Vitalistic Organisation

Evolving Engagement

Quadrant 2	Synchronous Strategy		Defined Design	Quadrant 3

Clarity of Mission

We had noticed over time that when we discussed a person or family we hadn't seen for a while at our team meetings, they very often contacted us shortly after. So, we ran a little exercise to test this. We decided to print out a list of everyone who had been into our practice in the previous year.

There were about 23,000 total visits the previous year, and every individual person's name was printed out. The purpose of this exercise was to reach out and be attractive, maintain connection and extend an element of nurture – to look after the people who have entrusted themselves to us in the past. We all went through that list, and I'm convinced that even the act of going through it created an energy shift in our office that extended beyond our walls.

The Institute of Heart Math in Boulder, Colorado has published extensively on the non-local effects of focused attention, and I am sure that our experience was an example of such.

What happened next was fascinating to me! The number of people calling to book an appointment accelerated. People still came in on their regular schedules, but at the same time, people who hadn't been in for ages started showing up.

The thing was that we hadn't even got around to calling the people on the list. It seemed like they just picked up the message from the ether and in they came.

This envisioning exercise is enough to convince even the biggest sceptic of its power. This was not an isolated situation.

Having a clear mission for your practice members is foundational to your success. It is your 'true north', and is a critical component to your Attractive Practice Model tool kit.

Every person has their personal 'true north'. For the greatest leverage, each must be aligned to the practice's, as expressed in the diagram below.

Your Practice's 'True North'

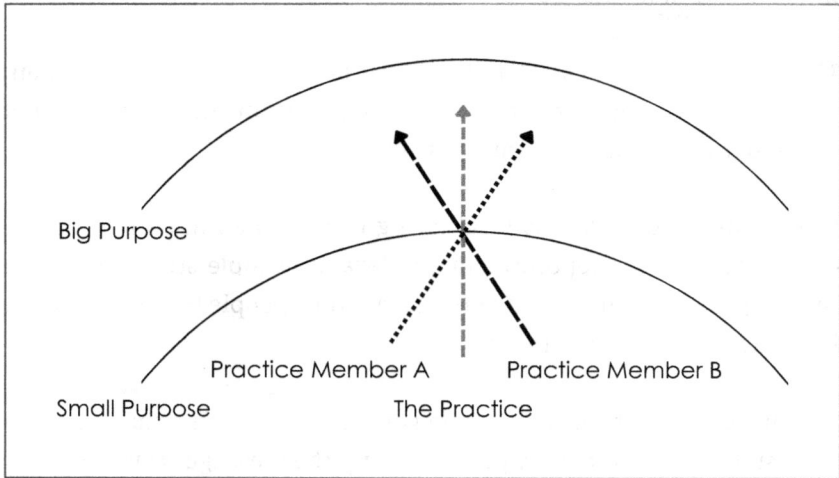

I can't tell you how many times I've had a crisis coaching call with someone whose practice has been hijacked by a big personality who seems to have changed the direction that they, the principal of the practice, had so lovingly and intentionally set. It hasn't occurred because of malice or malintent. It is simply that the mission of the practice was not big enough, and therefore a particular person, with a bigger individual vision, took it to where they wanted it. How do you create a mission that can hold to the 'true north' and withstand the impacts of big personalities?

The lesson here is that **THE MISSION MUST BE BIG**.

If your practice's mission is bigger than every person's mission, then they will find inspiration and purpose within the practice. People (team and practice members) will leave your practice when their mission exceeds yours.

That doesn't have to be a bad thing. Our drive to empower our team members has led us to sell off parts of our practices and build new ventures many times over the years. This was intentional: our goal was always to grow people until they could go out into the world with their own **BIG** practice vision to shape it in their own unique way.

It's a real challenge when small missions are outgrown by big personalities, which leads to conflict. When your practice members have a bigger vision than you and your team, they leave care. There is nothing left in your practice for them.

The bigness of your mission is the first line of defense against these problems.

Playtime

Practice your 'Team Visioning' exercise by reviewing the people who haven't been in for a while and discussing the things that you love about them. See what happens.

- What makes up the 'true north' of your practice?
- Where do the 'true norths' of each member of your practice team lie in relation to your practice's 'true north'?
- Throughout the week make an estimate of every practice members 'true north'.
- Do you have a 'Hijacker Proof' mission?

Summary

- You attract or repel people into or out of the practice by visioning.
- The power of having a clear vision is critical to the mission of an attractive practice.
- Every person on your team has their own personal 'true north', which must be aligned with the practice's 'true north'.
- The mission of the practice must be big enough to withstand the impact of big personalities.

- When the practice's mission is bigger than every individual's mission, they will find inspiration and purpose within the practice.
- People will leave the practice when their mission exceeds the practice's mission.

Global Problem

As humans we have an inner drive to follow our moral compass. When you look at the world you see things that are just not okay, by yours and your practice's values. Honestly, it takes only a few minutes of watching the 6 o'clock news to find global issues that are not okay. You and your team need to identify the ones that are *definitely* not okay by you all. Write them out in detail and make sure they are disgusting and repulsive. They must bring up the sadness, and possibly anger, within each team member. These are the things that you, as a team, agree to stand against.

An example from one of our clients' practices: *"there are hordes of people living their lives as victims. Ecological desecration of the planet costs them in sickness, misery, lost opportunity and decreased life expression".*

Local Solution

Once you have identified a Global Problem, get your team's agreement on what your local solution will be. The solution must align with your values and be actionable in your practice. This action will be a key component of your practice's mission.

An example from the client mentioned above: *"we reconnect thousands of people in our area with the lives of their dreams, empowering them to be, do and have their divine birth-right. We facilitate energetic shifts, which neutralise charge and increase awareness of their own infinite possibilities".*

Playtime

- What is the global problem that you see?
- What is the local solution that you are committed to?

Mission Statement

By now, you'll have asked yourself the following questions:

- What is your vision for the future of the planet, and what big changes will we see?
- What is the global problem that is going to be super-destructive to the world?
- What is our strategy to address this issue?
- What are we on a mission to deliver to the world?

These are some of the foundational questions that go into the mission statement (and I am sure that you will come up with more).

Go through the exercise of writing a full page of adjective-heavy, emotive vision-casting, and see what pops up.

The pathway to a magnificent mission occupies each quadrant of your business brain. Your mission, along with your purpose, creates your culture and is the driver behind your success. It allows you to create clear and concise direction, and ensures you can scale the practice. It also allows your team to get the same outstanding results that you do.

Playtime

- What is your practice's Vision?
- What is your practice's Mission?

The Team Centred Mission

The Team Centred Mission flows from your core values, your affirmational purpose statement and your practice mission, and addresses the identity of your ideal team.

Getting clear on this makes all aspects of operating your business so much more effective. Everything from hiring to training, reassessing, and firing is so much easier because the non-negotiables, aspirations and expectations are clearly written in this statement.

- Who are your team?
- Where are the gaps in your team (in both character and skills)?
- How do you want to grow your team?
- What area of excellence do you want to expand and improve upon?
- What strengths do you see in your people cause you to swell with pride?
- How do you want to grow and expand these strengths?
- What are your measures of team success?

When you clarify this vision, you will find the right people being drawn towards you. Ask yourself and your team to complete the following statements and you will be well on the way to having your Team Centred Mission completed:

We've talked about the big problem we're here to solve, the values through which we do it, and the big mission we are working towards. Every encounter with our team must be filled with this energy.

Make sure that you complete your Team Centred Mission. I would love to share hundreds of our clients' versions of this, but I guarantee that they wouldn't serve you, as you need YOUR Team Centred Mission, not someone else's.

Playtime

- What is your Team Centred Mission?
- Identify where your team is both congruent and incongruent with this document.

Practice Member Centred Mission

The Practice Member Centred Mission flows from your Core Values, Purpose, The Practice Mission and The Team Centred Mission.

The Practice Member Centred Mission identifies the four key parts of your relationship with your practice members. These people are your target market but more importantly, they are the people you are adjusting, as they reveal their inner perfection. These character traits are within your practice members, and it is your job to bring them out. Take the time to identify who these people are, what their character traits are, and what are you are doing with them and why.

It's highly likely that you will discover similar traits in this statement to your Team Centred Mission. I wonder why!

The categories of the Practice Member Centred Mission are the four Quadrants found in the Team Centred Mission.

For this one, also, you're on your own – I'm not going to give you a cut-and-pasted version of someone else's ideal practice member.

What I know is that when our clients nail their Practice Member Centred Mission, their practice becomes even more fulfilling, attractive and abundant.

Playtime

- Compile your Practice Member Centred Mission.

Summary

- A Mission Statement is essential for a business to create clear and concise direction.
- Your practice must be clear about your vision for the future, the global problems, your local solutions and your strategy to handle them.
- The Team Centred Mission flows from the practice's purpose and mission, and addresses the identity of your ideal team members.
- The Team Centred Mission helps with hiring, training, and firing by providing non-negotiables, aspirations, and expectations.
- The Practice Member Centred Mission flows from the practice's Purpose, Mission and Team Centred Mission, and identifies the four key parts of the relationship with practice members.
- The four key parts are the ideal people, what they do, the effect that the practice has on them, and the evidence seen within them.

Attracting people into your practice

Unless you practice in a remote outpost you will have huge numbers of people around your practice who need your services. You will also have some people who really want your services. And you will also have many people moving towards you, who know they need and want your services, but have other priorities right now.

The challenge in attraction is in getting people to warm towards your ecosystem and subsequently take the leap into your practice, engaging with your magic.

There is a systematic process to attracting people, as follows.

The Four Essentials to Attracting People

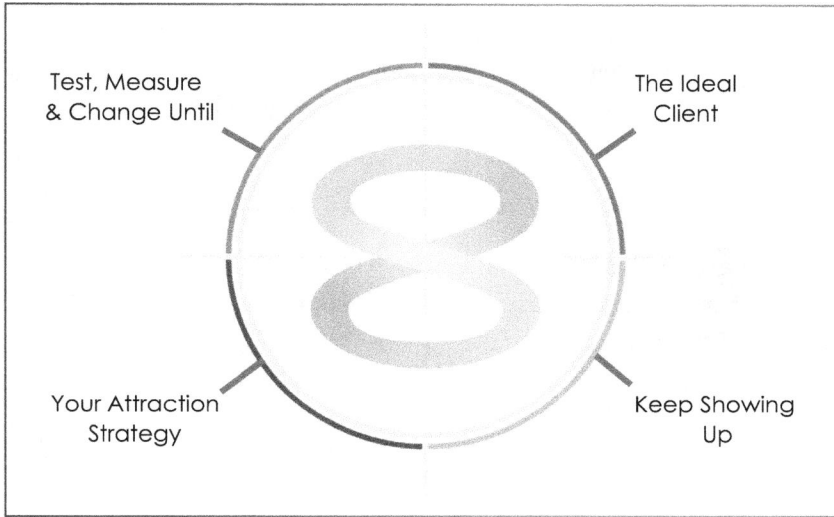

Test, Measure & Change Until

The Ideal Client

Your Attraction Strategy

Keep Showing Up

Q1 – The Ideal Client

Now that you are clear on your purpose, and you have your target market clearly identified, you can look at your message.

Heart-driven practitioners are driven by the compulsion to serve; they are compelled to share their message with the world. They often make the mistake of thinking that their service is for everyone. On one level, this is true. You probably *could* help every person, but in fact, you don't have the resources, or the bandwidth, to perform such super power feats. Every person has a different set of needs, wants and desires, so which of these do you choose to interact with?

People live in little bubbles and their filters of perception do not extend far beyond their bubbles. For example; a person with a diagnosis of 'cluster headaches' will pay attention when cluster headaches are mentioned, whilst a person with a diagnosis of 'tension headaches' will not.

Your message must, therefore, 'scratch their itch'. This is a real challenge when you know that your offering can benefit the whole person, no matter what ails them, but remember that when it comes to attracting people, you must speak to them directly. This means going inside their bubble and hitting that part needing attention.

Playtime

- What are the 'bubbles' that you love to serve?
- List three possible messages that speak directly to people inside each of these 'bubbles'.

Q2 – Your Attraction Strategy

For your practice to grow you must be constantly attractive to your practice members.

Remember, Practice Members are either working into or out of your practice at all times.

The list of things you can do to attract people is endless. And it's not about doing all of them. Try choosing three activities for your primary attraction vehicles. Some examples of actions you can take, both internally and externally, are:

Newspaper Articles, Press Releases, Columns, Print Advertising, Local Television & Radio Commentary, Magazine and Local Industry/Trade Journal Contributions and Advertising, Yellow Pages, White Pages, Online and Physical Directories, School Newsletter Columns, Advertising, Schools, Clubs, Groups, Events, Seminars, Fairs, Fetes, Shows, BNI, Gyms, Antenatal, Midwives, Corporate,

Organisation Promotions, Sponsorships, Lectures, Welcome To Our Area Packs, Demonstrations, Shopping Centre Promotions, Screenings, Letterbox Flyers, Welcome To The Neighbourhood Door to Door Meet and Greets, Brochures And Business Card Distribution, Direct Mail, Telemarketing, Cold Calling, Messenger Chats, Billboards, Posters, Shop-a-Dockets, Advertising on Taxis, Buses, Trains, Cinema Advertising, Facebook, Email, Website SEO, Sandwich Boards, Building Signage, Car Signage, Community Events, Window Displays, Merchandise, In-Office Video, Rolling PowerPoint, Displays, Brochures, Photo Boards, Testimonials, Fridge Magnets, Stickers and Tags, Linked In, Named Promotional Gifts, Charity Events, In Office Balloons, Blimps, Inflatable Figures, Plane Banners, Skywriting, Uniforms, Name Tags, Competitions, Fish Bowl Campaign, Surveys, Open Days, TikTock, Appreciation Days, Sign On Days, Orientation Days, Trading Sprints, Different Hours, Networking Functions, Strategic Alliances, Books, eBooks, Checklists, Infographics, Prizes, Giveaways, Referral System, Loyalty System, Bonuses...

This list goes on. There are so many things that will attract people to your practice. It is simply a matter of getting organised, getting off the couch and doing your specific things.

While there is a myriad of things that you *could* do, make sure that you only commit to those things that you *will* do. At Quest, we suggest that every two months you decide on the few things you can complete in the upcoming six weeks, leaving a couple of weeks for catch up or rest before taking on the next eight-week block of activities.

If your current focus is on attracting ideal people into the practice, create a clear path forward to take those people from 'cold' to 'warm' to 'ready to rock' practice members. Nurturing those who are moving towards you must be done with the long term in mind. Make sure that these people are getting all the sustenance they need – but not too much and not too frequently.

The roll-out of your attraction system is governed by your strategy. You may like to think of it in four parts:

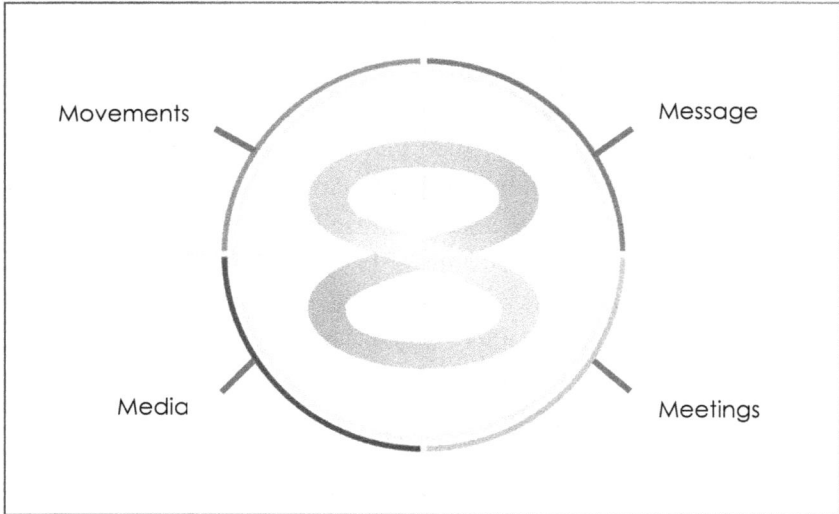

The Message: What is the message to be delivered every month?

The Media: Which media platforms will you use? What content will be given, and when?

The Meetings: There are face-to-face meetings to be held, either one-on-one or one-to- many. What are they and when?

The Movements: Every month there will be local, national, or international activities or events that resonate with your message. You can ride on the back of some of these. Which will it be?

Identify who the Messenger will be, what the Media channels will be fed about the message, what Meetings you will conduct (physical or online) and what the major Movements you wish to associate with (for each respective month) are.

We suggest that you get your Attraction Strategy sorted in November each year. Allow the time to think through the best placement and timing of events, and make sure that your team are all in agreement about their contributions to this plan. Lock it in and have agreements around when articles and postings are made and by whom.

Going forward, the current month's attraction activities should be finalised by the last week of the previous month. It also helps to have videos and social posts prepared six months ahead, so maybe schedule two video shoots a year.

MONTH	MESSAGE	MESSENGER	MEDIA	MEETINGS	MOVEMENTS
NOVEMBER	DESTINY	JS	1. 2. 3. 4. 5.	CREATING YOUR OWN LUCK NEXT YEAR?	Melbourne Cup - Tues Nov 3rd
DECEMBER					
JANUARY					
FEBRUARY					
MARCH					
APRIL					
MAY					

Q3 – Keep Showing Up

It's said that 90% of success in life (and in practice) is in just showing up.

Inflow is relative to outflow, so keep the units of information flowing out. This will create units of information flowing in. Remember, you cannot out-give the universe. This is not a passive thing. Just fixing up your website and running a few social posts doesn't cut it. It is a full immersion experience. The more touch points you have, the better the results. Remember, you are either growing or you are dying, so just keep showing up and be one of the few chiropractors who know the 90% rule.

Q4 – Test, Measure and Change Until

You cannot manage what you don't measure. The market is always changing, and this change is reflected in your results. Thus, it is vital you know what is working *now* so you can decide what to do *next*. Make sure that you have someone (preferably not you) to run this aspect of the business. You need to know the metrics but you don't have to do the detail.

Test and measure on a regular basis, and be willing to change until you get a satisfactory result. Remember, your practice is always broken. There is always something that could be better. There's always a new challenge/opportunity.

Playtime

- Get your Attraction Strategy sorted for the year and populate it.
- Commit to a constant outflow of content from your practice.
- Decide on the data points you are going to measure.
- Appoint someone to co-ordinate the attraction activities.

Summary

- Your attraction strategy should focus on constantly attracting and being attractive to practice members.
- Clearly identify your ideal practice member and tailor your message to speak directly to them and their specific needs.
- Practice members are either moving into or out of your practice at all times.

- It is important to get organised and focus on the things that can be done effectively with your current resources.
- Track progress and measure success.
- Make someone responsible for internal and external attraction.
- A good attraction strategy is a combination of the right message, the right medium, and the right offer.
- Attraction strategies should be flexible and adaptable to changing conditions.

Internal Attraction

The internal function of attraction is facilitated by the message that your attraction strategy has identified for the month. This sets the tone of the practice and is consistent with the internal and external events, outreach, content, and target market.

When your whole practice gets on board with the vibe of the message, it has far-reaching results.

Make sure that your message for the month is expressed well in the newsletter, which becomes the blog. It also gets expressed in the practice decorations, the talks, meetings, internal events, themes, offers, talking points, whiteboards, blackboards, kids colouring in, etc.

Sharing the results practice members have achieved is a great way for fellow practice members to discover the width and breadth of chiropractic's capabilities.

Try displaying an 'Our People Speak' folder, filled with testimonials from your practice members, in a prominent position in your reception area.

As stated before, every stage of a person's journey with you should ooze attractiveness in your practice's own unique style.

Playtime

- Create your monthly themes for the next 12 months.
- Download the 'Our People Speak' template, populate it and display it prominently in your reception area.

External Attraction

External attraction technology, commonly called "marketing", evolves quicker than the printing press can deliver a fresh load of books. This book addresses the concepts and principles of how to develop and run an attractive practice with ease, not the details and tactics of external attraction. We cover those within our coaching program, where we can make the necessary adjustments and changes as required.

On-line Presence

The old world of analogue data some of us grew up in didn't include the demands of online presence. However, in today's world it's a necessity. Social media marketing is par for the course. As chiropractors, we are no strangers to the demands and restrictions of health regulators, which can scare us off from risking their wrath. Yet we do need to make our attractive selves present, outside our bubble.

Practitioners getting the word on chiropractic 'out there' has always been necessary. We have never had third-party interests paving the way for us. B.J. Palmer, the developer of chiropractic himself, said, "Early to bed, early to rise, work like hell and advertise." So, the mandate to market ourselves has been present right from the start. It is the ethos our profession has grown up with.

In nature, first we sow seeds and then we reap. It is only in this post-modern society that we expect to reap without sowing. You need to sow the seeds. All things take time.

You must keep imparting your knowledge and wisdom to your community, even when it seems to fall on deaf ears. You never know when something will 'pop' for someone. It may be an example you give, a reference you make, or a different viewpoint you provide that will cause a person to take pivotal action.

To know and not share is a sin of omission. Please give and give generously.

It is important, at this juncture, to consider the big question, "What is your media?" The media you use is determined by where your ideal people hang out. Different demographics inhabit different platforms, so check out where your people express themselves and go there. You don't have to be on every platform. And remember that people and trends are always moving and what worked yesterday may not work tomorrow.

Search

There are people specifically looking for information relative to your topic. They want what you have and will come towards you when you let them know that you have it. Search engines and keywords will attract these people to you, so make sure you liberally spread the bait throughout your outflowing content. This calls for Search Engine Optimisation (SEO), which you can either do yourself, if so inclined, or outsource. Either way it must be done.

Interruption

Interruption marketing is about popping up in front of people when they are cruising along minding their own business. The strategy is to get into their feeds and the places they are searching, or areas that they may visit. This usually involves providing a pattern interrupt, something that grabs their attention and diverts them away from their original reason for being there. You will have been subject to this type of marketing, when you found yourself being lured by an interesting subject or offer that caused you to click away from your original purpose. This is an interruption to your initial reason for going online.

Methods of External Online Marketing

1. Free Marketing

You are a publisher and the more content you publish, the greater the opportunity for it to land and draw people towards you. There are essentially two types of free marketing, Random and Targeted. Both these methods can use either 'search' or 'interruption' strategies.

A. Random

As a publisher, you produce content on your publication channels (Facebook, Instagram, LinkedIn, TikTok, etc). Through these, people get to know you and like you and want more of you. The more real you are with people the more they are drawn to you *if* they resonate with you.

The purpose is to engage and share your valuable content, not just to teach, tell and sell. Really focus on solving people's problems; every three or four content pieces, make one an offer or a call to action. This is a very low-key approach. It is essential to maintain the balance between problem-solving and selling. If content is too heavy in the selling department, readers tend to disengage.

This process builds authority and draws people towards you and your practice. This is the essence of trust.

Make sure that you apply a high reward/low risk strategy by giving them lots of free stuff (newsletters, PDFs, video courses, Checklists, how-to's... etc). Do what you can to easily give them an immediate outcome, and they will want more.

When people are interested in you, they will go to your website. Many think that a website is all you need – this is far from the truth. A website is like an electronic calling card. It's not a place for you to tell the world all that you know.

People will land on your website for various reasons and they have their trust radar on high alert. The most commonly visited page on most practices' websites is the About Us page, especially if you have videos of the practitioners explaining why they do what they do in a passionate way. Many people will read your Google reviews to see what others are saying about your practice, so make sure they are being populated regularly.

People want an attractive experience on a website. Keep in mind your ideal people when designing it. Page layout, accessibility, colour palette and content must reflect the authority and the personal touch that exemplify you and your practice. These are all necessary components of a well-functioning website.

Some people will be there just to get your contact details because they've been referred to you. When they show at your practice, make sure they tell you the exact pathway they used to contact you. For example, the referral is stated as Google. In fact, a friend's recommendation lead to Google, and then to your website, which caused the person to call or make an online appointment.

Always ensure you have your Contact Us above the fold, and that you are able to collect contact details of the site visitors by offering a taster of you and your services. This allows you to continue the relationship by building your database.

Remember, the majority of people aren't ready to buy right now, so above all, make sure they have a pleasant experience, while at the same time making it easy for someone to make an appointment.

So, the Must Do, Must Have four essential pages are:

- Your Q1 page: the Opt-In page.
- Your Q2 page: the Thank You page, with a short video inviting them to register for a webinar.
- Your Q3 page: the webinar on how to do something.
- Your Q4 page: the offer of a short video course for them to learn more. This will include a call to action to reach out to you for care.

B. Targeted

Here we have a specific audience with a specific issue. The **more specific** you are, the **more engagement** you will get. Most practitioners think they can help *everyone*, but there's no such person as *everyone*.

Here, it's time to *get really familiar.* Go through your Client/Practice Member Centred Mission and develop your ideal practice member profile. Give the person a name and occupation and do a Google search on that name for the person who matches. Making up a collage of that fictitious person, along with their personal story, goes a long way to making your perfect practice member a tangible reality.

Who is this person? What is it that bugs them and how does that affect them?

You can narrow it down by running a campaign around, say head-aches. *But* this is not enough. How about if you call out those who have left-sided headaches? That makes certain people say, "That's me." And maybe you can even take it to the extreme, which some of our clients have done with great success. It could be something like: those who have left-sided headaches and are females who love surfing! I guar-antee this approach will appeal to certain people, who will say a very loud, "That's me, I need to see you."

One of our coaching clients ran a test on this notion. He chose a given problem, knee pain, and advertised in social media channels that he could help this issue. He got a pretty good response. Then, to test this ideal community idea, he advertised to the same population through the same channels for the same spend and the same timeframe, his services for *left* knee pain. The stats went ballistic. The simple act of being specific targeted a group of people who were more attracted be-cause he was speaking directly to their problem.

Paid Marketing

When you are paying for the ads, you must know specifically where your potential clients are hanging out.

This is where you *must* know *who* is your *who*, as we described above, otherwise you are wasting your money.

Now you know who your ideal practice members are, what they look like and where they hang out. The job now is to reach out to them and their 'look alike' audiences, who are those who follow the same people and are in the same groups, clubs or sports, etc.

There is no shortage of your people seeking your care in your com-munity. Marketing to them has never been easier (or cheaper) than now, so make sure you have a system that attracts your ideal peeps into your practice whenever you decide it's time to run a campaign.

One point here is that it takes a while for the social media bots to learn about you and your offering, and to gather your audience. We suggest you run a campaign for about three months for the best results.

Playtime

- Decide on your marketing strategy for the year ahead.
- Decide on which activities you will keep in-house and which get contracted out.

Tracking

Every person you attract into your sphere of influence must be nurtured and tracked. Make sure that you pixel (tag) those who engage, and retarget them with sequences of emails, videos, and other content pieces.

This tracking process moves them in a funnel to a landing page where you will offer them something of value. It could be a checklist, an exercise, a video, a white paper, an e-book, or the like.

Call To Action

To help people, you must get to consult with them. Often practitioners are reluctant to ask people for their custom, money and time. To help people the most, you MUST have them come in to see you.

Do whatever it takes to make it easy for the potential practice member to reach out to you. Many government regulators have strict rules around the ways you can attract people. Ethical bribes such as discounts, time sensitive offers and testimonials will certainly motivate people to take action but make sure that it is legal in your jurisdiction.

Partnership Marketing

Partnership marketing can be physical or online. This is where you enter into Joint Ventures or Affiliate relationships. When these commercially based arrangements are around products, equipment or consumables, they must be vetted regarding legality with your regulators.

The purpose here is not to address those relationships, it's to look at how you can develop mutually rewarding partnerships with those professionals in your area.

Often practitioners think that other practitioners and allied professions or industries are 'the opposition'. This is not true. Yes, these people, businesses and industries often have similar objectives and outcomes and yes, they often have your audience. But does this mean that they are in 'opposition'?

Maybe the fact that they have your audience could be a plus that allows you to reach out to mutually learn and share something new and different. This gives you and them credibility and authority.

We see many of our coaching clients expand their practices on all levels when they shift their mind-space around this issue.

Take the time to identify the players in your area who are in the same (or maybe even a different) 'sandpit' as you. Approach them and ask them to come to your practice and show you what they do. People love to share that which they are passionate about. Most are very happy to come along.

Through this outreach they get introduced to your practice and it usually follows that then they want to find out more about your offering, and in turn introduce their audience to you.

Not only have we used this strategy to build ours and our clients' practices, we have attracted other professionals who have ended up moving their practices into our building because of the mutual benefits.

Potential partners on many levels are all around you. Invite them in. Relate to them. Educate them and be educated by them, and enjoy the untold riches that flow to you and your practice members by the increase in value of partnership marketing.

Testimonials

When we relocated to a new area in which we knew very few people we got busy meeting the locals. As a chiropractor with an interest in cranial work, I thought it would be cool to develop a relationship with a dentist who had similar interests. It was a difficult assignment. I discovered that most of the dentists in our area were 'drill and fill' oriented and didn't have a holistic view of their profession.

The short version of a long story that spanned several years is that I found a dentist who was interested in upping his skill levels. I introduced him to other dentists and chiropractors in distant places, which ultimately resulted in him getting right into dental orthopaedics in a chirodontics model.

The end result was that his practice grew exponentially. He moved into our new professional building. We attracted many other professions and services into the building. Mutual referrals grew all practices over many years, serving countless thousands of people in our area.

Playtime

- Create your Marketing Strategy for the year ahead.
- From that Strategy, decide which activities you'll keep in-house, and which will be contracted out.
- Clarify who your potential partners in your community are.
- Create a strategy to go out and attract potential partners into your network so that you all serve and grow together.

Summary

- Online presence is a necessity.
- Your online presence should empower, inspire, and make your community and your practice members think differently about health and optimization.
- You must give generously to attract people to your practice.
- It is important to determine where your ideal clients spend their time and focus on those platforms.
- Search engines and keywords can attract people specifically looking for information related to your practice.
- Interruption marketing is about grabbing attention and diverting it towards your practice.
- There are two types of external online marketing: free and paid.
- Free marketing can be either search or interruption.
- The two types of free marketing are random and targeted.
- Paid marketing can be done when you have your organic marketing working.

Your Attractive Culture

Attracting people *into* your practice is just a small part of building a sustainable practice. The external processes we have discussed should be there but cannot be relied on forever. They are good to turn on and off when you have new providers joining your team, but the real momentum in your business comes from its attractiveness and its ongoing impact and contribution to your community. When this is working you will have a steady stream of new people lining up for your care.

The one thing that must remain constant, though, is that you, your team and your practice are presenting an attractive option to practice members on an ongoing basis.

So, let's have a look at what is needed to create and maintain an attractive culture for your practice members.

The Journey

Every person under your care is a unique individual on their own journey. You must choose whether you will be a casual event along their path or whether you will walk their path alongside them in a relationship, as you both ascend to realise your higher selves.

Most people lurch from one crisis to another; they don't have a strategic approach to their lives. Using the metaphor of the Journey, you have the opportunity to bring the cause/effect relationships of life to people's attention. Then, when they reflect upon their journey so far, they'll have a greater appreciation of what it takes to get to where they want to go.

When we work towards attracting the right people to our practice and journeying with them on their individual paths of ascension, they can experience the true transformation that you offer – but it does take time.

Thoughts of magic cures and instant results pale
when people realise that their current problem has
been many years in the making.

The Journey metaphor helps people to understand the cumulative effects of stressors interacting with resistance over time. Once they understand this dynamic, they can see why adjustments must be applied repeatedly over time, in order to facilitate a new normal for their brain and neurology to comprehend and embrace.

> *"I want to let you know that I've had a really awesome week. I've just finished my shift, in which I had some really cool, deep interaction with two clients. They both watched the Regenerative Care video, and they're getting the whole chiropractic journey on a level which I've never really experienced with clients before.*
>
> *So, I just want to thank you and the team at Quest for all the hard work you've done over the years to create this concept and its associated products. I've found it absolutely magical, transforming and really helpful for my career. Thank you. Happy Saturday."*

Adrian

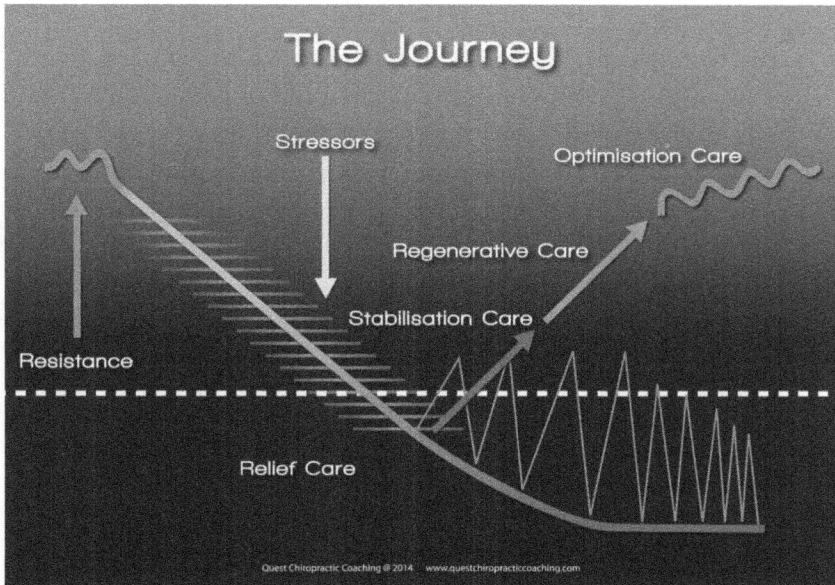

The Journey

Stressors
Optimisation Care
Regenerative Care
Stabilisation Care
Resistance
Relief Care

Quest Chiropractic Coaching © 2014   www.questchiropracticcoaching.com

People will ascend to a higher level of living if you give them the opportunity. It begins with showing them a model they can understand. The Journey model is just that. Use the Journey in all phases of your practice – it makes a huge difference.

Playtime

- Watch the Journey video for an understanding of the Journey.
- Order a Journey Poster for every adjusting area.
- Download a Journey graphic.

Summary

- Attracting people to a practice is important but not enough for sustainability.
- An attractive culture for practice members must be maintained.
- Journeying with individuals on their unique paths of ascension can lead to true transformation, but it takes time.
- External processes are important but cannot be relied on forever.
- Attractiveness and the ongoing impact of a practice are key to sustainability.
- An attractive culture must be maintained.
- The Journey model is a way to bring cause/effect relationships to people's attention.

Quest Procedures for Lifetime Care

The Quest Procedures For Lifetime Care is the simple structure your practice members are looking for to remind them and guide them on their journey. Here you have a specific map for your clinical process from the initial welcome of the new person to the various touch points that present in a lifetime of care.

This came about from trialing what works in ascending people to a higher level of health, happiness, and self-responsibility over many years in hundreds of practices.

As chiropractors realise, when they don't choose to spend the energy mapping it all out up front, they will end up spending that energy plus a whole lot more chasing their tails. They experience frustration and stress, because they (and their practice members) don't have certainty, clarity, and a way forward.

Have you ever sat and listened to an entertainer who kept hitting the wrong notes, or perhaps a comedian who only nailed one in three jokes? You stop listening from a point of relaxation and peace, don't you? You start bracing yourself inwardly, ready to give a sympathy clap or laugh. How likely are you to return to that club?

Imagine now that you are a practice member entering a chiropractic practice for the first time. They are running very late. They have mislaid the information form that you completed online the day before, so you have to fill out a new form. The CA is distracted by phone calls and requests from others as they are attending to you. Everyone seems to be chasing their tail. You hope the chiropractor knows what they're doing, but you are sort of bracing yourself. You enter the adjusting room in a defensive state. The chiropractor must now put you at ease.

When something is unfamiliar or disorganised, we seek safety. On the contrary, when we are welcomed by the familiar and the organised, we relax. We breathe out. We sense that here, it is okay to trust.

The Quest Procedures For Lifetime Care (QPFLTC) allows your practice members to rest with the knowledge that you've got them covered and you know what you're doing. You know that your care is beneficial across all ages and stages of life. But how you engage people seamlessly and easily in that journey may be something that requires work.

In this book I have selected some of the key processes we use to 'move the needle' in this journey of creating attractive practices. They allow you to create great momentum in your practice with ease.

So, let's take it from Day 1, the onboarding process when that new person first arrives.

The First Contact Reframe

The first contact with your practice has a huge impact on your relationship with your people. It is a critical time and one that you will have difficulty repairing if you mess it up.

People have their own idea of what your profession is and does, either through experience or by hearsay. It is very useful to interrupt people's patterns of thinking when they first arrive, so they don't just stay with their preconceived notions.

Your identification of who and what you are was discussed in the chapters on Core Values, Purpose, Mission, etc. The first contact is a great place to show your point of difference in your unique and natural way.

Make sure that your first contact with a new person is impactful and interrupts their normal patterns. From the initial intake form through to the time the person leaves, make sure that the experience is a WOW experience.

The Your History Form

The 'Your History' form is a critical form, not just because it captures essential information, but because it takes a person back into their history and demonstrates that things from the past are relevant to what is happening now. This plants the seeds of chronicity, which are essential to a person understanding the complexities of long-term care.

In this form, we don't ask the 'normal' questions that other practitioners do. The questions in this form are disruptive. They ignore the typical "problem", "disease", "pain", "source" and "intensity" questions and go for the timeline. Questions like, "Was your mum's pregnancy with you wanted?" cause people to have a neurological 'flip-out'. This speaks to a person's sense of self, identity, belonging and purpose. And you bet it always makes people think and can often lead to new awareness.

> *I remember a gruff truck-driver called Max coming in one day. He came in wearing the Australian truck driver's uniform – stubbie shorts and a blue singlet. "I want my back fixed, mate," he said before pointing at his lower back. "Just here. By the way, that question on the form is rubbish, mate."*

> *"Which one?" I asked.*

> *"That bit about how I was born. It's rubbish."*

> *I didn't bother to defend it. I simply joined his model of thinking. "Yeah. Seems like it. And, you know what? Every event in our past has an impact on who we are now".*

> *He shrugged. It was a half-hearted agreement, and I went through with checks and subsequent visits as usual. To the outsider, it might not have seemed earth-shattering.*

Now, fast forward 10 days. He came in to the practice. He had a humble air about him. He said to me, "I couldn't get it out of my mind." Then this giant of a man started to tear up and, still speaking in short, gruff sentences, he said, "Yeah. I haven't spoken to mum for years. So, I called her and asked her about my birth... she immediately lost it... she burst into tears... She didn't want to get pregnant... She poured out the whole long story. Apparently, we both nearly died at birth.

Yeah. I didn't know that. It's made me think differently about her and we're going to catch up next week."

Talk about a pattern interrupt. That question created a paradigm shift. It created a pivotal point in his life's journey. From wanting a quick fix for his back problem to still getting regular checks and adjustments in order to optimise his life expression some 11 years later, when he moved out of town.

Playtime

- Design your introductory forms to create pattern interrupts for your new people.
- Download an outline of the Quest Procedures For Lifetime Care

Summary

- Building a sustainable practice involves continuously presenting an attractive option to practice members.
- Each person under your care is on a unique journey.
- Walk your practice member's path alongside them.
- The Journey model is a useful metaphor to bring life's cause/effect relationships to people's attention.

- QPFLTC is a structure that guides practice members on their journey, providing certainty, clarity and a way forward.
- The QPFLTC has four areas which relate to always attracting: Inspiration, Management, Delivery and Reinvention.
- The first contact reframe is critical in creating a good relationship with practice members.

The ADIO Visit

ADIO (as every chiropractor will know) stands for "Above, Down, Inside and Out", representing a workable process of your practice's 'brain', based on the *in8model*®. The construct underpins the four stages of a practice member's interaction, from Agreement through Discovery, through Investigation and the Opportunities that follow.

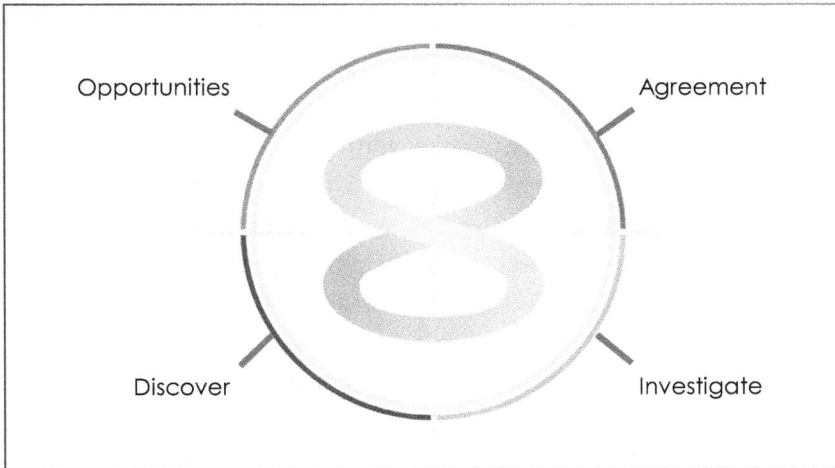

Q1 – Agreement – the 'Yes/Yes consult'

The 'Yes/Yes consult' is a simple yet profound process that forms the foundation of a lifetime of management by agreements in your practice.

Start every new person consult with an open-ended question like, "How can I help you?"

The person will instinctively tell you what is at the forefront of their mind. For example, "I want to get rid of (problem)." Now, let's assume that this is <u>not</u> the 'real' problem, but potentially the *key* to uncovering the 'real' problem.

Instead of jumping in right away and digging for the details of the 'thing' that brought them in, how about letting the 'thing' that *really* brought them in to come to the surface?

When you hold the space without talking or diving in with more questions, typically one of two things happens: either the person starts to tell you how their life is affected in much more detail, often with emotions coming to the surface, or a long and uncomfortable stare-off ensues. The former outcome usually occurs when a person is given the opportunity to go a little deeper. It will be something in their life that they value, but can't do because of the 'problem'.

This is their real reason for seeking your care.

Acknowledge the person with, "Yes, we have had success with (their problem). To find out how well we can help you, what we need to do is (list all the things that you will do on this visit and the next). Is that okay?"

You are looking for a wholehearted, congruent "Yes" from the person.

This is the first of many agreements. When we start a relationship with small mutual agreements and fulfil them, both parties are more inclined to enter into bigger and longer agreements in the future.

This builds trust. Every stage of a person's journey with you must be underpinned by mutual agreements. Agreements build trust and trust is attractive.

Playtime

- Get your Yes/Yes consult designed and scripted.

Summary

- ADIO is the workable process for the first visit.
- The Yes/Yes consult is the foundation of a lifetime of management by agreements in your practice.
- Let the person's real reason for seeking care come to the surface instead of immediately digging for details of the problem they mention.
- Look for a wholehearted, congruent "Yes" from the person.
- Avoid dumping your knowledge on New People.
- Every stage of a person's journey with you must be underpinned by mutual agreements.
- Agreements build trust and trust is attractive.

Informed Consent Builds Trust

Informed consent is not only a legal obligation. Informed Consent can educate, inform, and build trust. It's about making sure that the practice member is aware of what you are about to do at each phase of care. It covers the known upsides and downsides of every phase of care. It also must be specific for every phase of care:

- When the practice member moves into the first stage of care which might be a specific problem they need Informed Consent.
- When the practice member moves to the next level of care, which might be more about regeneration, they need Informed Consent.
- When they move to Maintenance care, they need Informed Consent.
- When they move to Optimisation care, they need Informed Consent.
- When they haven't been seen for a certain time period, they need Informed Consent.

- When they change care levels (i.e., after an accident, injury, operation, even pregnancy), they need Informed Consent.
- When you are doing a technique that may be considered on the fringe, they need Informed Consent.
- Depending on your regulatory body's requirements, they may need Informed Consent for 'non-therapeutic hugs' (which is the case in Australia!)

The bottom line is that every phase of care is an opportunity to practice empathetic, evidence-informed, transparent communication with your practice members. This deepens the trust and increases the attractiveness of your practice.

Playtime

- Get an Informed Consent drawn up that includes not only the downsides but also the upsides of care.

Summary

- Informed Consent educates, informs and builds trust.
- Informed Consent ensures that the practice member is aware of the reason for each phase of care, along with its benefits and risks.
- Informed Consent is necessary for every phase of care, including specific problem-based care, regeneration, maintenance and optimisation care, or when a fringe technique is used.
- The PCA forms a part of Informed Consent.
- It is required when there is a change in care levels or a long gap between appointments.
- Every phase of care presents an opportunity for empathetic, evidence-informed and transparent communication with the practice member.
- Practicing informed consent can deepen trust and enhance the attractiveness of the practice.

Q2 – Discovery

The Case History Reveals Chronicity

Commonly, people seek your expertise thinking that the 'problem' is as old as the first time they felt it, and that it should be resolved in a similar timeframe. This is faulty logic that is, unfortunately for humanity, being perpetuated by the instant results mindsets supported by our current health system.

The Your History is different. It is discovery of their true STORY – it is their history. You want the gems that people don't think are important. The only way to get this is to ask them questions they aren't anticipating. People expect "age, sex, occupation, chief complaint." They don't expect questions pertaining to the meaning and quality of their lives.

This is why the first document that new people receive is the Your History form. This is the WOW moment that causes people to be distracted from their normal patterns and know that you have something different going on.

After getting agreement through the Yes/Yes, they enter the Discovery part of the first visit. You now have the opportunity to take them on a process of exploring their past, based on what they have written in the Your History form.

This takes an attitude of intense curiosity.

Dig for chronicity. Go way back to their earliest times. They may not have answers to the questions, but it will make them think and possibly research the information later.

In the first part of the Discovery phase you are expanding on what they have reported. The person must understand their history is totally relevant to their future trajectory. If you are espousing healthy lifestyles, you want them to get that you are there for their life's journey; you are not a brief whistle-stop along the way.

Our coaching clients constantly record huge wins with people's care plan compliance by doing this simple step. Now it's time to unpack where the physical, mental and chemical stressors have been in the past and link them to patterns, regions and systems of their body that may be affected now.

Playtime

* Write up your history-taking procedure.

Summary

* The Your History form is given to New People to encourage them to think deeply about their lives and provide important information.
* The Discovery phase of the first visit involves exploring the person's past, including chronic stressors, and their impact on physical, mental, and chemical health.
* Unpacking the person's past and linking it to current patterns, regions, and systems of the body can lead to greater compliance with care plans.

Your Snappy Systems Review

Focusing on digging deep with people, you will be faced with a number of challenges, such as rapport, trust, memory, language limitations and cultural differences, to name a few.

The systems review is a complete journey from head to toe covering every functional system. This is so valuable in conveying to the person that you have an interest in their whole body and mind, not just the limited context they think you are good for.

Keep it short and snappy and make it understandable. You may frame it like, "(Name), let's get a snapshot of your history. I'll go through your body's systems, and I want you to tell me if you've had any problems or issues with them at all, even back into your childhood – OK?"

As you go through every system don't just name the system – eyes, nose, ears, head, etc. – as the person may not relate to a given problem in their past to these labels. You need to be more specific and use their language. For example, ears – hearing problems, infections, glue ear, swimmer's ear, tinnitus, Meniere's disease, etc. This triggers people's memories; in their book, they didn't have ear infections, they had swimmers' ear.

This is a quick-fire process that reminds people that they have encountered breakdowns in their bodily systems in the past. These have been accommodated for, but the memory still resides in their body. Knowing this, they are prepared for the fact that, later down the track, they may revisit this old dormant problem and have a chance to really deal with it.

Playtime

- Get your Systems Review scripted.
- Gather a list of examples of associated symptoms to ensure that you reveal the deeper issues.

Summary

- Digging deep with people can be challenging due to rapport, trust, memory, language, and cultural differences.
- The systems review covers every functional system from head to toe. This demonstrates interest in the whole body and mind.
- Keep the systems review short and snappy and frame it as a snapshot of the person's history.
- Be specific and use the person's own language when asking about problems with each system. This will trigger their memory.

- This process helps people understand that they may revisit earlier breakdowns in their body during their care.

Q3 – Investigation – the Touch that Tells

Now that you have a deep discovery process sorted you are ready to dive into the hands-on stage of Investigation. Investigation is about your examination.

We see major breakthroughs in our clients' practices when they use the Investigation component of the first visit and go beyond the pain-based exams they were taught at university. Instead, they immerse themselves in the structural and functional exams directly related to their clinical application, and open up a dialogue that continues throughout their care.

Exquisite Exams

All too often our exams and tests are in conflict with our clinical objectives. We wish to take people on a journey of function and health, yet our focus and exams are directed towards disability and disease. Whilst it is important to cover the red flags of the presenting complaints and other complicating phenomena, it is important to direct our emphasis and people's experience towards the wanted outcomes.

Your examinations must be oriented towards your clinical actions. How do your exams add to your clinical knowledge and certainty?

People exhibit deficiencies in many ways and regardless of your clinical approach, it is worth assessing the person from a global to a specific perspective. Global assessments may include:

- **Standing**. People are biped and exhibit their ability to comprehend their environment in a standing position, so observe them in this position and test for stability.

- **Walking and Gait**. Observe coordination, balance and gait to assess cerebellar function.
- **Breathing**. Notice where they are breathing from, the ease and intensity of the breath.
- **Supine**. A person should be able to easily lift both legs and one leg at a time in a supine position.
- **Neurological**. The appropriate reflexes and neurological responses must be consistent with the person's presentation, age and stage of development.
- **Prone**. Assess relevant structural, neurological, and muscular tests.

Every touch and test of this investigation should convey a sense of interest, curiosity and wonder to the person. Remember, *don't* talk, other than commands. (It's okay to grunt, gasp, shake your head and give the occasional, "Oh dear.") *Don't* touch and tell. (You want them to feel the experience.) *Don't* give advice. (This is investigation time, not care or advice time.)

Playtime

- Review your investigation process and make sure it is congruent with your philosophy and delivery approach. Is it Exquisite?

Summary

- Investigation is the hands-on stage of examination after the deep Discovery process.
- New People experience breakthroughs in their understanding when exploring beyond the pain-based exams.
- Exams and tests should be oriented towards clinical actions and add to clinical knowledge and certainty.
- People should be assessed from a global to a specific perspective, including standing, walking, breathing, supine, neurological, and prone tests.

- Every touch and test should convey a sense of knowing and certainty to the person.
- During investigation, don't talk (other than commands), touch or tell, or give advice.

Q4 – Opportunities Report

Many chiropractors think that the pivotal visit of a new prospect's chiropractic experience is the report of findings visit. This is far from the truth. The first visit, as you have seen is a four-part sequence that sets the scene for ALL to come. The crowning glory of the first visit is the Q4 component – the Opportunities Report.

Having established agreement and uncovered some of the prospect's drivers, visited the person's intricate history with the Discovery process, and deeply investigated their presenting state way beyond their presenting complaint, you are now well placed to reveal to them a snapshot of your findings, way beyond what they anticipated.

The Opportunities Report is not a full report of findings. It is a demonstration that you have the skills to look way beyond the current issue and see solutions to problems they may have wondered about for many years.

The object of this visit is quite simple. After the preceding 5-10 minutes of grunting, sighing and other strange noises, you are now able to tell them more about them than they told you. When you do this, you take over the narrative. They must understand that the various 'issues' they consider to be normal need not be. All parts of their body are interconnected and you know what to do to sort it out.

If you were to hear this new person's internal dialogue, it would sound something like, "Yes, this chiropractor understands me. I've been telling other health practitioners about this for years and this chiropractor has just nailed it in five minutes."

They are now hopeful, excited and primed to turn up to the next visit and consume the Pre-Care Appointment and the Report of Findings that follows.

Playtime

- Go through your tests and exams and identify where this person will malfunction, especially in areas they've not told you about.
- Create a narrative of those things which will have repercussions, based upon your positive exams and observations.

Summary

- The Opportunities Report is the highlight of the first visit. It provides a snapshot of the chiropractor's findings beyond the person's expectations.
- The report convinces the new person that the chiropractor has the skills to see beyond the current problem and find solutions.
- The goal of the visit is to show the person that the issues they consider normal have a rationale and an interconnectedness, and that the chiropractor knows how to sort it out.
- The report takes over the narrative, and the person feels understood and excited to continue care.

Pre-care Appointment – Making the Journey Real

You may relate to taking a long drive with the children in the car. There are the inevitable questions as they sit uncomfortably still in the back seat asking, "Where are we going?", "When will we get there?" and of course, the most annoying one, "Are we there yet?"

Your practice members are no different. They must be forgiven for thinking that any health issue is just an isolated event – they just need to drop by your practice and get it 'fixed'.

You must provide them with context for their care. This involves showing them how they got to where they are now, and a logical pathway forward. People will stay with you as long as you provide them with a compelling future.

Before a person commences care they must complete an informed consent and part of informed consent is what we call a Pre-Care Appointment (PCA). This gives them the opportunity to question their own and society's current practice of treating the symptoms and putting up with 'normal'. It gives people a framework for designing their own healthcare journey by exercising the choices available within your offering.

The PCA is the second visit, and it takes the form of a short video. It can also be offered as a live presentation.

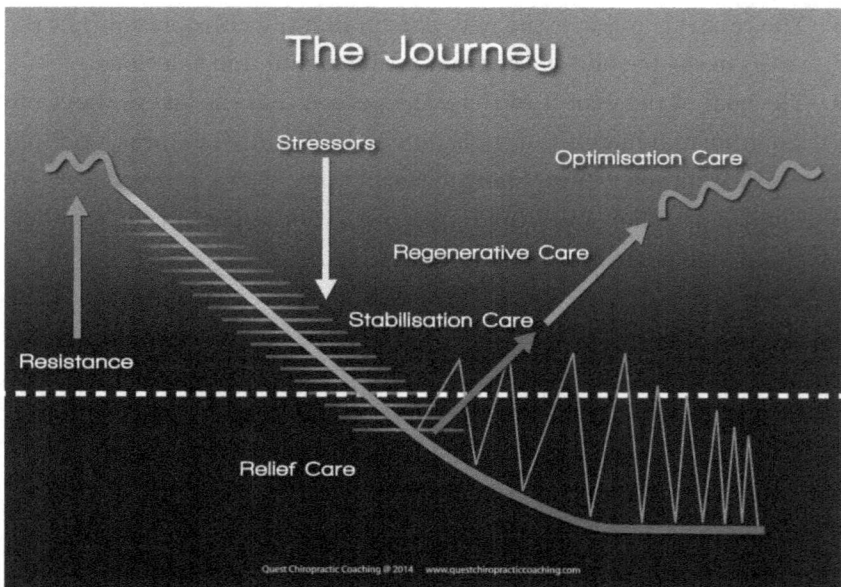

The PCA is an absolute game changer. It builds on the Journey model instigated by the Your History form, the Yes/Yes that set up agreements, and the Discovery and Investigation that you did on the first visit. The PCA is a pre-frame for your Report of Findings. Here you will make your offering for optimal care.

Once the person has seen the PCA, the Report of Findings is simply a 'fire drill', taking very little time. The new person understands the options and just needs a few details around frequency and the financials of care, and they are good to go.

Playtime

- Find out more about the Pre Care Appointment.
- Get your PCA up and running in your practice.

Summary

- People often view a health event as needing just a one-time fix. They need context for ongoing care.
- The pre-care appointment (PCA) is an important part of informed consent before starting care.
- The PCA is the second visit and involves a short video or live presentation to educate people on their healthcare journey.
- The PCA builds on the first visit, sets up the offering of the report of findings and previews the educational events to come.

Report of Findings – the Biggest Anti-climax Ever

Many practitioners see the Report of Findings as the opportunity to show and tell the potential practice member all that they know on the subject of chiropractic in one big brain dump.

For many practitioners the Report of Findings (ROF) is a Sales Event: the *Attraction* part is all over and the practitioner is trying to *Convert* the new prospect into their offering. The focus is around selling, convincing, negotiating, *'closing'*, and having people 'buy' programs.

In contrast, the gentle approach of the Attractive Practice Model has a different intent and process.

The key components of the ROF are:

- To offer a very basic summary of exam findings and how they cross-correlate with your other findings.
- To show the person their x-rays, photos, scans and other instrumentation results, orienting them to their normal/abnormal anatomy, bones and discs, etc.
- It is simply a matter-of-fact 'fire drill', designed to give recommendations for the optimal duration and frequency of care.
- The person makes their decision based on this information.
- The chiropractor gives the personalised Journey Report to them as a record of the agreement reached.
- If the person rejects the ROF, it may be necessary to close the case file and find another chiropractor who better meets their needs.

Playtime

- Roleplay your ROF.
- Get a professional Journey Folder.
- Get Report of Findings support documents

- Brainstorm the exceptions that exist or may present for your practice.

Summary

- The Report of Findings is a quick 'fire drill' after the PCA.
- The person just needs details on duration, frequency and finances for Stabilisation Care.

Regenerative Care Appointment – the Journey is in Full Swing

Your Practice Member's journey through Stabilisation Care will have provided many Light Bulb Moments (hopefully, on every visit). They will have been steadily gaining an increased awareness of themselves and their future possibilities, on all levels, which may have been denied them up until entering your practice. When they complete Stabilisation Care, they come to the next juncture of the journey – the Regenerative Care Appointment.

The drip-feed system of table talk and demonstration during Stabilisation Care, covered in the Deliver section, prepares the person for the information presented in the Regenerative Care Appointment (RCA) video. This equips them to make decisions regarding the next stage of their life's journey. These will be presented in the Progressive Report of Findings.

You will see many epiphanies occur with your practice members when they view the RCA as Adrian's practice members did.

"I wanted to just let you know that I've had a really awesome week. And I've just finished my shift and had some really, really cool, deep interaction with a couple of clients. They've both just attended their RCA and they're getting this whole chiropractic journey on a level which I've really never experienced with clients before. So I just want to thank you and the team at Quest for all that hard work you've done over the years to create the product, because I found it absolutely magical, transforming and really helpful for my career. Thank you."

Playtime

- Check out the Regenerative Care Appointment.

Progressive Report of Findings

Care agreements extend from one phase of care to the next. As the person ascends through the phases of their care the mutual trust will be increasing, provided both parties complete their side of the deal.

By the time a person has gone through the Stabilisation Care phase they will have been learning and noticing that significant changes are happening to their body, mind and ways of thinking.

The Progressive Exam and subsequent Progressive Report of Findings is an analogue marker of the person's ascension in care. If the Stabilisation Care process has been followed properly, the person will have already made their mind up about their future direction in the practice, so this visit, much like the Report of Findings visit, is just a confirmation of direction and leads to a new agreement being made.

The Progressive Report Of Findings will give the person information about where they are up to with their care. Tests, photos, and examinations are compared to the originals.

Regenerative Care over a substantial time frame (possibly years) may be indicated. At each juncture of Regenerative Care a new Progressive Exam is done and a new Progressive Report is given, detailing the options going forward. These will be either to Regenerative Care or to having their case closed (or any other option you may offer them). If they are continuing with Regenerative Care an understanding and agreement for the duration and frequency of the next phase of care will be reached.

Playtime

- Identify and brainstorm the exceptions that exist or may present in your practice.
- Drill the Progressive Report of Findings.

Summary

- The Progressive Exam and Report of Findings serve as markers for the person's progress and direction in the practice.
- The goal is to reach an understanding and agreement for the duration and frequency of the next phase of care.

Scheduling – the Practice Member's Personal Journey

No practitioner has a crystal ball revealing the future, so there are no magic formulas for frequency or duration of care.

Scheduling of care then depends on the softer generalities that are on offer. The practice member's *Outcomes* are one. If you were a swimming coach and a young person came to you saying they wanted to learn to swim, you may ask, "So, what are your outcomes?" An answer may be, "I want to swim so I don't drown." This would engage you in planning and recommending the 'waterproofing' swim class, which may be a month-long program for the average beginner. Likewise, if that young person said, "I want to be an Olympic gold medallist", this would bring a very different recommendation, involving tens of thousands of hours of lessons and training, specialised diets, mental training and so forth.

Likewise, the *history* and current *state* of the young person wanting swimming lessons would make a difference to the recommendations. The point here is that recommending the length and duration of care is an exercise in heuristics. Like climbing a mountain, where you would have a strategy about the path you will take, and estimate the rest or camping areas along the proposed ascent. You can never plan the exactness of the journey, which rock to put which foot on, and so forth.

The same goes for your care recommendations. You can take into account the outcomes, the history, the present state, lifestyle, occupation, stress levels, etc., and estimate the approximate time to reach certain milestones, but you must be willing to have it 'set in jelly'. This is why you chunk care into segments. People don't then have to choose the 'lifetime' engagement. They can take bite-sized pieces along the way towards their objective.

One size does not fit all, but my observation is that most professionals in health care suffer from the 'messiah complex'; they underestimate the time it may take to see a practice member attain the desired level of ascension.

Frequency – Consider what habits a person's physiology has adopted. When something has existed for a period of time it becomes 'normal', and even when your actions liberate a greater potential, the 'normal' memory wants them to revert. Herein lies the need for repetition over time, to re-educate the human system into a 'new normal'.

Duration – The human being has a great ability to regenerate within the limitations of tissue. Given enough time, we have an incredible opportunity to regain lost function. Being mindful of this and giving the practice member the chance to choose are important parts of your care recommendations.

Don't short-change people by not recommending enough time to achieve their needs, wants and dreams. You do them a gross disservice and create reputational damage for your practice, rendering it less attractive for that person and the community.

Successful scheduling depends upon checking in with the person's progress at regular intervals. Be as systematic as you can with this.

Be mindful of the highest good of the practice member at all times, provide the best recommendations for care, continually inspire people with the possibilities that await them, test and measure along the way, check in regularly and always over deliver.

Playtime

- Get clear on your clinical rationale for scheduling.
- Make sure that you and your team understand why you do repetition over time.
- Check-out the ROF Support documents.

Summary

- There are no set formulas for the frequency or duration of care.
- Scheduling of care depends on mutually desired outcomes, history, current state, lifestyle, occupation, stress levels, etc.

- Care recommendations are an exercise in getting agreement on the time necessary for you apply your clinical skills.
- Recommendations are a time, not number-of-visits, agreement.

Quadrant 2: Naturally Nurturing

The 8 Strategies Of The Attractive Practice Model

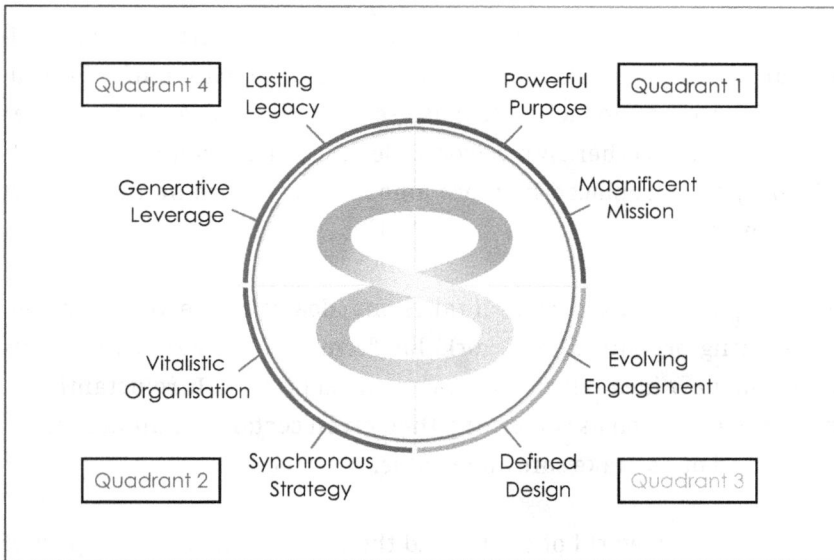

I once heard a mother lament the differences in parenting styles. She and her husband were both working from home and taking turns parenting the kids. "When I'm taking care of the kids, its structure, structure, structure. I want them to have things to do – predictability and stimulation. So, I have their day mapped out with mealtimes, chores, reading practice, outdoor play, messy play, gardening, art and cooking, right up until when their dad takes over and I work.

Then his method of parenting is to build a fort out of cushions in the lounge room and let them go nuts.
And he's the favourite parent!"

What we are seeing here is the classic nurture of the Q2 part. The mother wants the children mentally stimulated, emotionally safe, able to thrive and learn within the structures she has set up for them. As this mother is to child, so the Q2 part is to the attractive practice. Dad might be able to stir the imaginations of the kids by hyping them up on box forts and playing pirates and kings (the Q1 and 3 parts typically played by the practitioner), but without Q2's nurture, no one eats, reads, paints, cleans or has any clothes to wear.

Ideas are born, romanced and amplified in the Q1 part. The possibilities are endless and the heart pounds with anticipation of a new future. If there was no facility to make sense of those ideas and to gather the concepts together into a workable form, they would wither and die, only to be replaced by more amazing new ideas in a very short space of time.

Thanks go to the Q2 part, as it takes one idea at a time and fits it into an existing organised and workable form. The Q2 part will always greet the new idea with resistance and skepticism. It reluctantly accepts the intrusion as something that, given certain conditions, could be worked on to make safe and usable.

Welcome to the world of the Q2 and the land of nurture. This part of your practice is about taking the big picture ideas and philosophies and integrating them into a nurturing structure that enables your practice to function like a well-oiled machine.

Q2 is where all that visioning and inspiration in the enigmatic and big-picture-thinking Q1 becomes organisation, control, operations, and strategies. We call it the Nurture Quadrant because it needs those essential elements to give space for an organism to grow. The action and intention of Q2 is to nurture this organism (your practice), and ensure this 'baby' succeeds.

To Be or Not To Be the CEO

Many erroneously think that, for the practice to grow, it is the job of the practice owner to either assume the role of CEO and/or be the head of the Nurture department. For most, this is a recipe for frustration, loss of passion and a redirection into other side hustles.

Let me ask you this: can you show me a dedicated practitioner who loves caring for their practice members being over-the-top excited to attend to the administrative demands of the practice? Do they love spending hours in paperwork, compliance, reporting, researching, information processing, wages, paying the bills and general management? It is a rare practitioner indeed who is drawn to that.

Chances are that you began your journey into and through this profession to have an impact on people and make a contribution to the world, not to be the ego-driven, nit picking, bean-counting Boss.

Now, this is not to say that many practitioners don't find themselves in this position. Commonly we assume this position by default. As the practice grows and we learn by trial and error how to manage things, we put the proverbial choke around our neck. This creates significant blocks, as we become the 'log-jam', finding everything coming back onto our plate. Overwhelm and loss of passion ensues.

One of the most common desires of strung-out practice owners seeking our coaching services is to go from hobby to business. The challenge is to be in love with being a chiropractor and applying ones skills to holding all the juggling balls in their hands, to the chair of the board, leading their world-class team and doing what they love. It is possible to move towards a vision that is bigger than any one of the team. It is attainable when they come together to form a functioning and flowing business brain.

The key to this is *not* in ascending yourself to the CEO role.

Instead, it is to design your practice to reflect a vitalistic process that is inherent in the way nature works and your brain and body functions. Let's explore Vitalistic Organisation in a brain-based model.

Playtime

- Do you want to be the CEO, or the Chair of the Board?

Summary

- The Q2 part is responsible for creating a mentally stimulating and emotionally safe environment for the ideas and philosophies of the practice.
- The Q2 part is responsible for taking big picture ideas and integrating them into a functioning and organised structure.
- It is not necessary for the practice owner to take on the role of CEO.
- The key to success is not in ascending yourself to the CEO role but in designing the practice to reflect a vitalistic process as a decentralised network.
- The role of the owner is to focus on what they love while inspiring their team towards a vision that is bigger than all of them.

Strategy 3: Vitalistic Organisation

The 8 Strategies Of The Attractive Practice Model

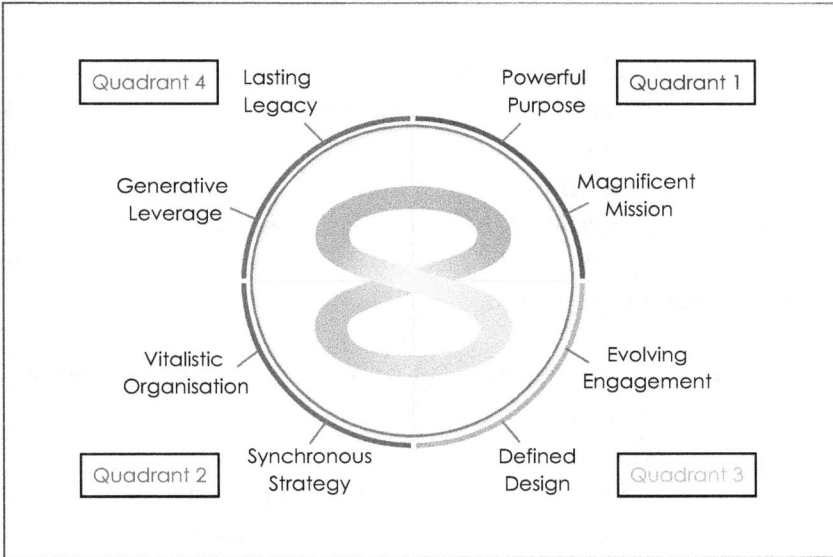

Quadrant 4	Lasting Legacy	Powerful Purpose	Quadrant 1

Generative Leverage

Magnificent Mission

Vitalistic Organisation

Evolving Engagement

| Quadrant 2 | Synchronous Strategy | Defined Design | Quadrant 3 |

Just like the human body has life expressing through its physical parts in a decentralised network, so too does a practice. While we are inspired by the free-flowing inspiration and connection of the 'right brain' of our practice, we must have the 'left brain' organising and sorting with precision in order to ensure that things get done. Both of these components are necessary for wholeness.

All parts must integrate for the whole to function with integrity.

The net effect of a well-functioning organisational part of your practice is the conservation of energy. Organisation is the function of removing the impediments and interferences to success that cost *you* in time, money, and energy.

Dealing with disorganisation is such an energy consumer. It saps the passion of the practice. Just think about the impact of stress on your team's attention and focus when they are 'putting out fires', chasing things that should have been done, finding information that should have been better organised, and a myriad of little things that have a big drain on efficiency and effectiveness.

Now, imagine your practice's Nurture part operating from a place of empowerment. Your practice is organised in alignment with its values and purposes. Everything is in its place and people know what is next in all processes. The necessary management numbers are always available at the press of a button. Your service delivery is well oiled, consistent, and predictable, and your practice members are happy with the great service and superb clinical results.

There is certainty, consistency, and predictability at all times. It frees up energy. Think what you can do with that. You can spend it in creative endeavours growing your business. You can spend it playing golf, lying on the beach, or catching up with friends to replenish your emotional tank. You can take a holiday/vacation. Take a week or 10 off. Spend time with your kids. Go to a seminar. Your time is yours because the practice just works from above down and inside out.

Playtime

- Look at your practice and do a quick audit on the energy leakage.
    - How organised are we?
    - Does every aspect 'run on rails'?
    - Is there a predictable flow for your practice members?
    - Do your scheduling and billing processes work smoothly?
    - How well do you take care of your records and information?
    - Is your education system seamless?
    - Are your care protocols duplicable?
    - Are your outcomes consistent and predictable?

    ◦ Do people step through your front door and feel as if they are being looked after by a team who knows exactly what they are doing, and do it easily, on purpose, effectively and efficiently?

Summary

- The human body and your practice are both decentralised networks, with the "left brain" organizing and the "right brain" inspiring.
- Both components are necessary for wholeness.
- Organization removes impediments to success and conserves energy.
- Disorganization saps the passion of the practice and has a big drain on efficiency and effectiveness.
- Empowered, well-organised practice with consistent and predictable service delivery frees up energy.

Ideas Into Order

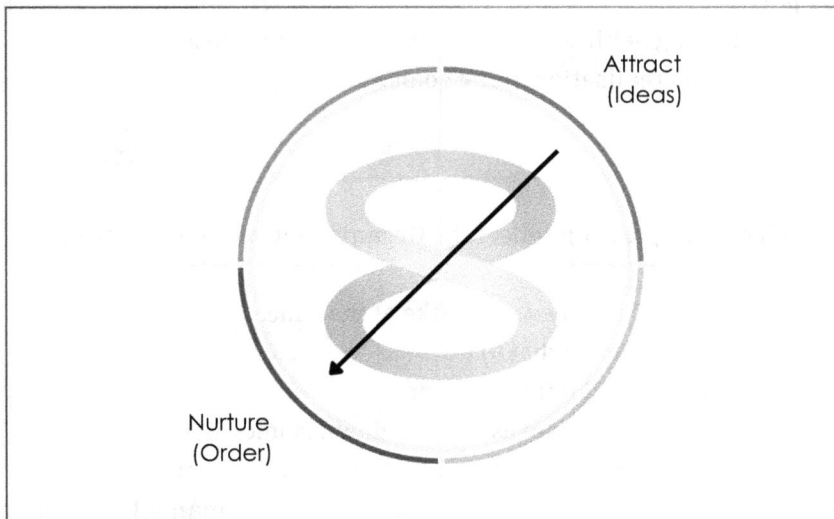

Attract
(Ideas)

Nurture
(Order)

In Q1, we saw how important it was that everyone knew they were in the right place. In Q2, this idea is transformed into clear and practical ways in which that sense of knowing is achieved.

People are attracted to your practice, either as a practice member, associate, or CA. They are then empowered through the Q2 function to know *where and how* they fit into this tribe. There is nothing worse than catching on to the vibe and vision of a practice, but not knowing how you can engage or contribute. Over time if this isn't addressed, it becomes frustration and disengagement. Hence, nurture is vital.

When we are building an attractive practice, we hire what we lack, both in terms of skills and perspectives. I say all this because oftentimes, a typical chiropractor (often being strong in Q1 and Q3) won't get excited about analysing where a business is thriving and where it isn't. They won't light up about creating reports and accountabilities. But someone will, and when you find them, your life becomes easier because wherever the attractive person goes with their big thinking Q1 part, creating a beautiful mess of possibilities, a person who oozes Q2 comes along behind and shapes the mess into structures, strategies and hence the realisation of the goals.

Playtime

Which of the following reflect the Organisation of your practice?

- We do things the way we feel like at the time.
- My team just know what to do.
- My team do what I tell them to do.
- We have some procedures written down (somewhere).
- We have great written policies and procedures for the front desk.
- We have a complete policies and procedures manual for every function in the practice that is continuously being updated.
- We have an Organisational Storyboard with allocated roles.

- We constantly update and refer to our Operational Storyboard.
- We have a specific job description for each position.

Control

Much like a mother works to get her baby into routine so they have enough sleep, food and stimulation to grow and thrive, so too does the control aspect of the Nurture part allow the business organism to grow and thrive.

A common misconception is that we must control our people. In the Attractive Practice Model, you control the systems, and the systems control the team and business. It's an important distinction to make, as when you control a *person,* you limit their capacity to grow and thrive. When you control systems, and the systems do the work, the people maintain their sense of freedom, personal agency and innovation, and therefore rise to the occasion.

Good systems control means you don't have to think about where to file the papers, or where to find that receipt, or how to measure that month's business flow. We put in the hard work behind the scenes so that all can run smoothly. Here, with the control aspect of Q2 doing its thing, the people in the business are free to set their sights on attracting, delivering, and expanding.

Earlier on, we introduced the concept that the attractive character, the principal chiropractor in a practice, is usually the big picture person. They are not best placed to be the CEO. Rather, Q2 houses the CEO functions. They control, organise, mobilise, train, and propel the business forward, dotting the 'i's' and crossing the 't's.

Let's think about the word "control". We know that words are important, as they build up the culture set in Q1. The words you use determine the practice that you have. Do you have staff or a team? Do you have patients or practice members? Do you have outcomes or ascension aspirations? Do you retain or attract? These are important distinctions, and they are central not only to the development of your culture, but to the process of managing according to values.

We have already mentioned the retention vs. attraction dichotomy. Attractive practices are not here to retain people – to forcibly hold them. Attractive practices are here to attract people and go on a journey with them for as long as they can add value, inspiration, alignment and be attractive to them and their life.

We can't force people to engage with the amazing power of the natural world. We are not serving them well or allowing their highest potential to be manifest when we try to make them conform to our ideas.

Frankly, we are not here to convert people from one state to another. We are here to journey with them, and through that journey, enable them to connect with their inner intelligence in their own unique way.

How well and with how many people you can do this depends on how well your practice's Q2 operates.

Karen is the kind of woman who always has activity surrounding her. And as a classic Q1 preference, she is always at the centre of it. She is lively, magnetic, a gifted healer and a wonderful chiropractor.

She is also incredibly disorganised. Over the time I've known her, she has made a wonderful adaptation and accommodation to her Q2 part.

Having been an associate overseas and then returning to Australia, Karen joined a practice as an associate. After spending some time practicing there, she decided the time was right for her to make a stamp on chiropractic under her own name and in her own way. In true Karen style, she never shied away from a crowd. She went to a gym and began to practice there, essentially by herself. She had one girl come and help her for a few hours per week, but it was primarily a solo effort with very little organisation.

She got her feet wet in this setting, and it was a necessary start for her, because she soon realised something profound: you can be the most amazing chiropractor and have the most amazing venue and technique, but if you don't have the nurture there in terms of organisation, structure, systems and procedures in place, things will constantly fall apart and must be reinvented.

She identified this and, rather than trying to force herself into an unnatural role for her, brought someone in who did Q2 really well. This allowed for structures to be built to carry and facilitate the growth.

And grow she did. Soon she bought her own building and shifted into it, and now has an associate in the practice. It's going gangbusters and is booked out way ahead. That is the result of filling that gap with the Q2 part. It makes all the difference to the superpowers we have as practitioners in terms of the philosophy and delivery of what we do. When we get someone in who can keep us organised, it's a match made in heaven.

Karen didn't have to do the organising herself. She didn't have to work on her weaknesses or become the CEO she was never meant to be. She has learned to find people in who can assist her with this function.

If you want your practice to thrive, you absolutely need to have a thriving Q2 department. It doesn't have to be you who performs this function, but it must be the right person, with a nice balance of power and force.

- Is there enough control in your practice?
- Is there too much control in your practice?
- Where are the gaps in the organisational parts of your practice?

Roles, Responsibility and Accountability

I have a strong Q1/3 preference, so administration and organisational control hasn't been my forte. The universe in all its intelligence hooked me up with Jackie. She is a wizard at all things Q2/4 related. I'm thankful for this; otherwise, I'm sure that I would have spent a lifetime in a world of possibilities and ideas that never materialised.

In our years of coaching chiropractors, the most common thing we see is lack of structure in terms of roles, responsibility, and accountability. It is here that stress and discord thrive.

We often find chiropractors loving what they are doing but bogged down because they are trying to keep all the balls in the air. They are repairing things, organising things, and making things happen because they are the only ones in the practice who know how to do it. This leads to burnout and resentment. They become dispassionate and frustrated with their team. This is endemic in the profession.

One of the great gems of wisdom gleaned along the way is this: make the roles, responsibilities, and accountabilities clear.

Too often we think that empowerment is about keeping things vague and letting people create their own possibilities. Rather, we use roles, responsibilities, and accountabilities to set the foundation. From there, the inspiration from Q1 flows through to the structure in Q2. We see the bases are being covered and recognise room for improvement in the way we deliver (Q3) on these responsibilities. From there, we can sit back and reflect on how we might expand and improve (Q4), and this leads back into Q1 for more inspiration.

But we can't do any of it unless we make those roles and responsibilities clear and have clear accountabilities. This doesn't necessarily mean a hierarchical structure. We encourage flat accountability structures such as the Storyboards which makes us accountable to ourselves and our teams. We celebrate when things get done on time or in an excellent way in order to create a culture of proactivity and innovation.

Playtime

- Make a list of roles and responsibilities for every team member.

Summary

- Good control is about systems, not people.
- Systems control allows people to maintain their sense of freedom, personal agency and innovation.
- The use of certain words can shape the culture of a business.
- Attractive practices focus on being attractive to people, rather than holding on to them and retaining them.
- Forcing people to conform to a certain idea is not serving them well.
- The right person should have a balance of power and force.
- Clear roles and responsibilities are important for accountability and success.

The Organisational Storyboard

The Organisational Storyboard featured strongly in Walt Disney's creative workshop and has been adopted in physical and digital format in many of the top companies in the world. The Organisational

Storyboard is an excellent tool to take your practice's nurture to the next level. It assists with accountability and organisational responsibility, and we see huge leaps in the practices that we coach when they get the storyboard up and running:

- It takes the focus off the person and personality and puts the attention on roles and responsibilities.
- It takes information out of one person's head and puts it down on paper (or whichever medium you choose).
- It creates accountability across the organisation.
- It shows where the gaps or overloads are.
- It makes sure that everyone is pulling together and moving forward.

You can do an Organisational storyboard regardless of whether you are a single practitioner or a chain of practices. It's all about getting those functions of the four Quadrants organised so that you can see what needs to happen and hold yourself and others accountable.

Remember that talent trumps time in the practice. Make sure that the right people are in the right roles on the Storyboard, regardless of their seniority in the practice. Yes, be ready to be held accountable by a 20-year-old if they have talent that you or the others don't have.

Organisational Storyboard

BOARD OF DIRECTORS - Vision, Strategy

OFFICE MANAGER - Strategy > Tactics

ATTRACT	NURTURE	DELIVER	EXPAND
KPA - New People	KPA - PVA	KPA - People Served	KPA - Revenue
Culture	**Organisation**	**Front Desk**	**Internal**
SOP	Story Board	Arrivals	Talks
	OP & P Manual	Telephone	Events
Branding	Rosters - Chiros and CAs	New People	Education
Aesthetics		Education	Adjusting Areas
	Human Resources	Departure	Scan Room
Possibilities	Hiring	Scheduling	X-Ray
	Meetings	Follow Up	Reactivations
Engagement	CAs	Case Management	Reception Area
Christmas Party	Chiropractors	**Clinical**	Library
Celebrations	Assessments	**CA**	Reading material
Social	**Plant & Equipment**	Philosophy	Our People Speak
	Computers,Printers and Software	Science	Photo and Notice Boards
	Printers	Communication	Overhead Boards
	Software	Technique	**External**
	X-Ray	Client Services	Website
	Security System	**Chiropractor**	Blogs
	Plants & Garden	Philosophy	Social Media
	Repairs & Maintenance	Science	Mailing List
	Cleaning	Communication	
		Technique	Conversion
		Imaging	Video Distribution
		Education	Speaking
		Research	Screening
			Finances
			Accounts Payable
			Accounts Receivable

This method of displayed thinking enables a practice to identify all of the chains of action and roles and responsibilities and ensure that every activity is written up in the Office Policy Manual. The flow of command comes from the vision and strategies generated by the owner or the Board of Directors, and may be delivered by an Office Manager. (We discourage titles like Office Manager as they reinforce a hierarchical model and tend to encourage Force instead of relying on Power.) In most practices the team create the Storyboard together.

As the Storyboard is being compiled, we recommend that you agree on the best people for each role, starting with the top positions of Attract,

Nurture, Deliver and Expand. The KPA's (Key Performance Actions) are the primary statistics for these areas. Following that, agree upon the individual centres of activity in the practice and agree on a person to be responsible for each.

Each team member then proceeds to write up any necessary Policy and Operations for one portion of their assigned area at a time, as described below in the Policy and Procedures Manual section. Allow time for this; it will always be a work in progress, but is well worth the time and effort.

Remember that a formatted business is a business that can be scaled without you.

Playtime

- Do a brainstorming session on what you are doing and could do in each of the four key Headers of your practice (Attract, Nurture, Deliver and Expand).
- Write down any possibility or thought that comes to mind.
- Eliminate those ideas which don't align with your values and purpose.
- Write up the shortlist of key activities under each Header.
- Under each activity identify what needs to be written up and by whom.
- Only allocate one or two key activities for each team member to write up at a time.

Summary

- The Organisational Storyboard is a tool for improving accountability and organisational responsibility in a business.
- It focuses on roles and responsibilities rather than people and personalities.

- It documents information and creates accountability across the organization.
- It helps identify gaps or overloads in the organization.
- It ensures everyone is working together towards a common goal.
- Talent is more important than seniority in determining roles on the storyboard.
- The Storyboard should be created, and key roles and responsibilities identified, by the team together.
- A well-formatted business can be scaled without the owner's constant presence.

Policy And Procedures Manual

The Policy and Procedures Manual has four main parts. I guess you're no longer surprised by the 4 Part thing. Yes, we want to have the policy or the procedure easily understood so we need to know the purpose of the procedure, the content of it, the description of how to do it, particularly the script, and then the exceptions or alternative ways of how we can make it better.

This leaves us with the four areas of Purpose, Procedure, Script and Exceptions.

The Policy and Procedures Manual Order

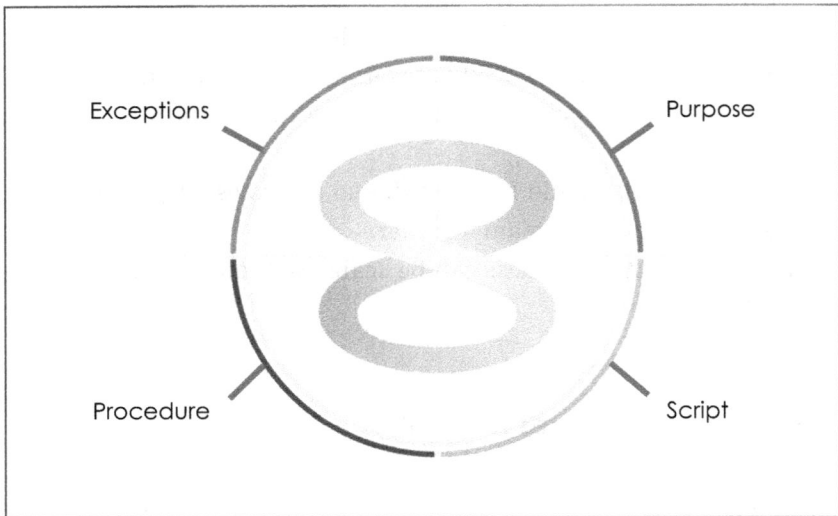

Exceptions

Purpose

Procedure

Script

The Policy and Procedures Manual is always in the process of completion. There are always reviews of the practice's activities, requiring alterations.

For those activities and processes that require addendums or links to third party information, e.g. government policies, instruction manuals and the like, we suggest you add an Appendix.

Playtime

- Identify who will direct the compilation of your Policy and Procedures Manual.
- Allocate every team member the task of one or two write ups at a time.

- If you want to short-circuit the time on this project, we have a Policy and Procedures Manual Template available.

Operational Storyboard

The second storyboard is known as the Operational Storyboard. This is a rough and ready whiteboard, constantly being added to and subtracted from. It's not a pretty site, but it is *soo* functional. It is a focal point of the Team Meetings. (See Team Meetings in the Delivery section). It is best located in a space that is accessible to your team. The Operational Storyboard has the 4 Quadrants as its functional units, and only features those ideas, activities, projects, or commitments that are relevant to the *current projects* of the practice. It will stop 'problem' talk and get the team focussed on action.

In contrast, the Organisational Storyboard, as discussed earlier, contains the reference for the entire practice's operations. It is detailed and specific. But, when it comes to the rollout of the current projects of the practice, we don't need the complexity of the Organisational Storyboard. We just need a template to keep us on track – where are we now, where are we going and what the next step is.

The way the Operational Storyboard is used is quite simple. The practice's Core Values are written around the outside; within that is the familiar brain-based model we call the in8model®.

Q1 (Top right) – Begin your interaction with the Operational Storyboard via a brainstorming session. Firstly, visit the ideas that are already on the board in this area, some of which may have been added since the last meeting. Now, seek new ideas in any area of your practice's activity, specific to the theme or projects you are working on in this 8 Week Leg. No idea is too stupid at this time.

Q2 (Bottom left) – The Q2 area houses the projects already underway, with a due date attached and people assigned. They report on the status of each current project.

Q3 (Bottom right) – The workable systems are transposed to the Delivery area. Projects that have reached the point where communication, team and delivery mechanisms need to be discussed are now dealt with. The new or amended procedures are written as policy.

Q4 (Top left) – Exceptions or suggested redesign to Policies may be listed here for discussion. There are no 'sacred cows' in this quadrant. It is the centre of robust discussion. The focus here is on expansion and doing more with less.

The Operational Storyboard carries the current key statistics. Q1 is numbers of New People, Q2, The Ascension Index (PVA) and Q3, Total Visits. Some practices list the Q4, Total Revenue, on the Organisational Storyboard and others reserve that for the chiropractors and the owners reporting.

The one number that features on this storyboard is the Critical Number that you are monitoring for all to see. For most chiropractic practices it is the number of checks and adjustments, for both the current period and year to date.

We do suggest that you create 8 week cycles of activity. Start the cycle, or Leg, as we refer to it, with an intensive session. Focus on the Quadrant/s that will move the needle the most. Establish the number of projects that you can realistically handle in the time allowed, and move them to the Operational Storyboard project system.

Playtime

- Get an Operational Storyboard made and installed into your team meeting protocol.
- Check out the Quest Intensive events for our coaching clients and apply to attend as our guest.

Summary

- The Operational Storyboard is a whiteboard, constantly updated in and between team meetings.
- It focuses on current projects and ideas, and directs the team's actions.
- Operations cover everything and anything having to do with expansion and congruence, consistent with the practice's values.
- The team should focus on a limited number of activities every 8 weeks and chunk for success.

Strategy 4: Synchronous Strategy

The 8 Strategies Of The Attractive Practice Model

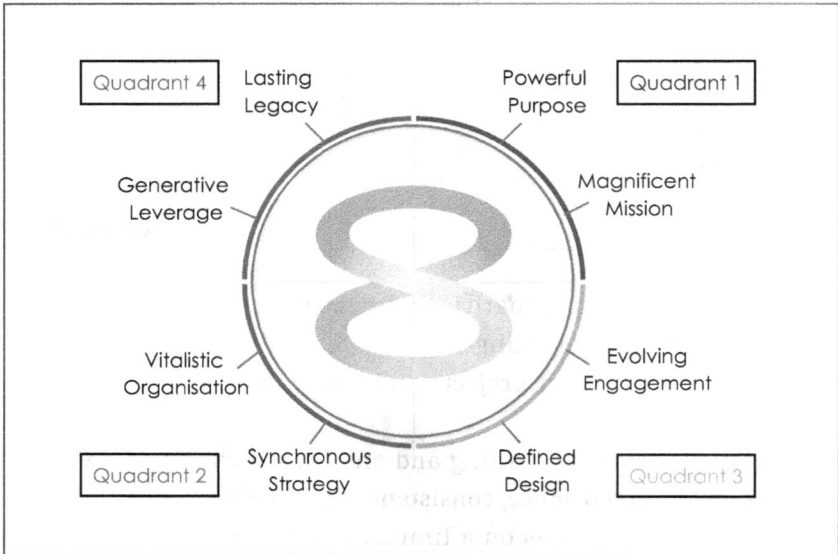

Joseph had been a big one for the 'flow of life'. He avoided planning anything because he felt that it stifled spontaneity and authenticity. He rejected protocols of care and insisted that he "wanted to make the system and techniques fit the person and not have the person fit the system and techniques." Every person had a different process, from times allocated to technique applications to payment amounts and methods. It was dizzying and his practice was not firing. He was disheartened because the practice members didn't use his services to the fullest extent. He was initially very resistant to creating a clinical strategy (let alone strategies for other aspects of the practice). He was a hard nut to crack, but as he developed the relevant strategies and the resulting tactics, things began to change. The inflow of new people increased in each of his practice work-flows; the ascension of people through the levels of care increased; the bottom

line improved significantly, and of course, his disposition upleveled beyond belief.

It seems that the more we prepare and practice for something, the more the right circumstances, situations, people, places, timing and events present themselves to us. It seems like the intention behind strategy, or maybe just strategy itself, is a prime driver of achievement. A mission remains a hope or a dream if there is no clear strategy to make it real.

When it comes to this area of Nurture, your practice's Organisation gives you your ability to assume Control. This then fires up the ability of your Operations, which in turn allows you to be strategic.

Strategy as another critical leg of the Attractive Practice Model, so get into strategic thinking mode. Come up with systems and procedures to provide a safe and familiar vessel for your practice members to navigate their unique experience with you.

The Quest Procedures For Lifetime Care is a strategic framework of application that gives predictable results. It has been tried and tested over extended periods of time in countless hundreds of practices. Your mission and clinical outcomes may be very different to other practitioners, so make sure you identify your values, beliefs, and purpose (which we covered in Attract), to ensure that your strategy is congruent all the way down.

Playtime

- What is your strategy for taking your mission out into the world?
- What is your strategy for hiring, training and upskilling your team?
- What is your strategy for nurturing your practice members so they have every opportunity to have a positive experience when they are with you?

- What is your strategy for those individual systems and procedures that ensure that the right thing happens, in the right way, at the right time, every time?

Summary

- Organisation enables control, which then fuels operations and strategic thinking.
- You need a clear strategy for taking your offering out to the world.
- Strategy is a prime driver of achievement, and a clear strategy is necessary to make a mission a reality.
- Identifying values, beliefs, and purpose is necessary to ensure that the strategy is consistent.
- Developing systems and procedures to provide a safe and familiar experience for practice members is essential.
- The Quest Procedures for Lifetime Care is a tried and tested strategic framework that produces predictable results.

Quest Procedures For Lifetime Care

Let's check in on the 4 Areas of the QPFLTC as they relate to Strategy. The QPFLTC is a sequence for taking each person on their clinical and educational journey of ascension in an attractive way.

Those notions that people hold about their health and life that are useful and producing results are supported. By the same token, those that are no longer useful are challenged. The intent of the QPFLTC is to provide people with an environment where they can experience perspectives different from their current worldview. Subsequently, their behaviours and the results they are getting will be more useful.

The QPFLTC Strategy

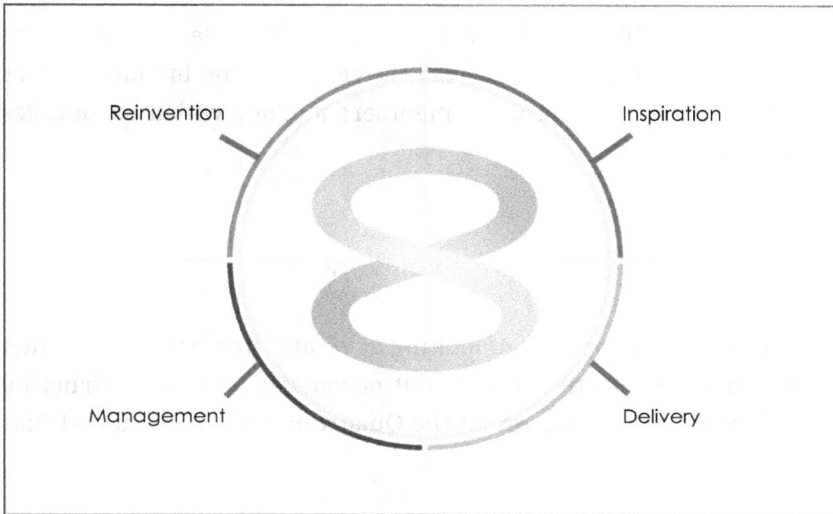

Reinvention   Inspiration

Management   Delivery

As noted earlier, each Quadrant of your brain (and your practice) performs a certain function, identified on the diagram above. Throughout this book we are cycling through Inspire, Manage, Deliver, Reinvent and back to Inspire as we ascend and grow.

Q1 – Inspire

People are innately curious. We daydream, fantasise and plan for things and times that have not yet occurred. This is the field of possibilities that inspires all people to move towards a lofty vision.

Q2 – Manage

The Management driver is the part that brings order and structure and enables your vision to be realised. It ensures that practice members are nurtured and supported in a predictable and ordered environment.

Q3 – Deliver

Being able to deliver on the promise, to provide order and structure in the process and to demonstrate the reality of the big idea creates a Wow factor in your practice members journey which encourages them to seek more.

Q4 – Reinvent

Reinvention is the process of looking at what is and has been created from a new perspective. It is about deconstructing, reconstructing and planting new ideas, which the Quadrant 1 picks up on and flies with.

Playtime
___

- If you haven't already, download the Quest Procedures For Lifetime Care now.
- Check off those strategies you have nailed and are happy with.
- Commit to creating those strategies you've not yet addressed.

Statistics – Measure the Quantity and the Quality

What you don't measure, you cannot understand and cannot manage.

Management by values might sound like it erases the need for metrics, but it's quite the contrary: it means we measure *differently*. It may actually mean we measure *more*. We measure the *how* and the *what* that pertain to our values. *How* do we achieve what we set out to achieve?

What Action do we take to move towards it, and *what* did we achieve when we did these things?

By measuring the how and the what, and connecting these to our values, we create a map of our progress. We measure the Quantitative *and* the Qualitative. Along with the numbers of New People, Quantities of Visits, Collections, Overheads and the like, we also address the Qualitative factors: how many of these people are part of our tribe, reasons for care, frequency and duration of care, satisfaction levels, contribution, etc.

The way we measure is as important as measurement itself. Around 40, I did my midlife crisis. Instead of buying a Harley, Jackie and I invested heavily in a chiropractic software company, packed up the three kids and moved to the USA. 1989 was the beginning of the personal computing era and we bought into a start-up in the newly forming software industry, about which we knew nothing.

It was a major learning experience. We were in a start-up organisation that was flying by the seat of its pants in totally uncharted waters. The measurement of success was solely quantitative. This led to questionable practices. Everyone's statistics were due on a Friday. If we didn't meet our targets each week, the company would have to close down. Simple, right?

This uncertainty and pressure created a culture in which everyone thought only of the deadline. It became a mad rush to make your benchmarks by Friday. This, for some, meant moving outside the values of the business to reach those targets.

Management by objectives such as this can accidentally create a culture in which we get conditional with our values to get to the 'magic number'. But in the long run, it compromises who we are as a company, or as a chiropractic practice, or indeed as a person.

Statistics are not, in and of themselves, the goal. Your goal is driven by something far greater. It is aligned with your mission, your beliefs, and your aspirational purpose. Make sure that your values remain front and centre as you go about the business of your practice.

Here, the true essence and beauty of the *in8model*® flow is put on show. This isn't an isolated section of the brain or the business, working away behind a desk and disconnected from the flow and energy of the business. Rather, we are flowing from section to section, bringing new life and structure, application, and growth as we go. Each part is present, needed, valued, and empowered to be its best.

We are picking up the values, vision, and language from the Q1 part, and using measurable tools to affirm these outcomes. These apply to three key areas (which we work through more thoroughly in the Quest coaching program). These three layers are equally important.

- They are person-related outcomes, such as quality of life measures or metrics for practice members' results.
- They are team-related goals that set up and measure personal growth.
- They are business-related outcomes that ensure you are tracking well financially and growth-wise, in accordance with your values and mission.

Here, the term 'management by values' is of utmost importance. What you measure and how you measure it should line up with the culture you are creating and the mission you are on. So qualitative measures are just as important as quantitative measurements.

Playtime

Decide on the key metrics you are going to measure and make sure they are both Quantitative and Qualitative.

Every eight weeks, focus on the Quadrant/s that need assistance. Eight weeks is long enough to move the needle and short enough to keep things fresh.

Keep the anticipated accomplishments realistic and attainable with your time allocation to the immensity of the task.

If you require help with this, we invite you as a guest to one of the Quest Intensives held online every 2 months. Contact us at <u>admin@questchiropracticcoaching.com</u> for your free pass to the next Intensive.

Summary

- If you don't measure something, you cannot understand it or manage it.
- Measurement should line up with the culture and mission of the organization.
- Management by values means measuring the how and the what that align with values.
- The way we measure is as important as measurement itself.
- Measuring both quantitative and qualitative factors creates a map of progress.
- Management by objectives can create a culture of compromising values to reach targets.
- Statistics are not the goal, but should align with mission, beliefs, and purpose.
- The Attractive Practice Model flow connects different sections of the business to bring new life and growth.

Quadrant 3: Delightful Delivery

The 8 Strategies Of The Attractive Practice Model

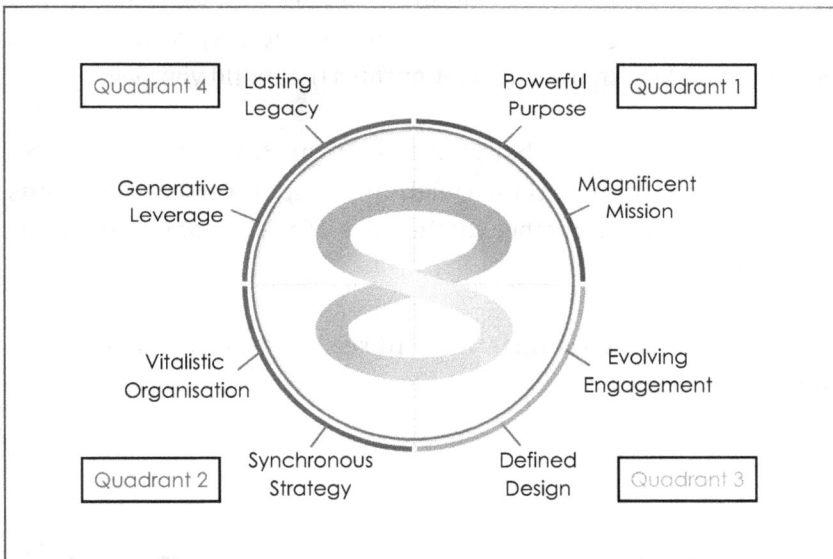

Your big ideas are conceived in Q1, ordered and organised into worka-ble systems in Q2 and then filtered into the practical delivery focussed function of Q3. This is where most chiropractors thrive. The practice member comes in. We connect with them. We check and adjust. We ask meaningful questions while planting positive feedback. We use the techniques we have spent years studying and perfecting to restore them to a state of ease and optimal function. The Q3 part of the chi-ropractor will stay up at night grappling with different cases and re-searching different techniques.

You could make more money in industry and commerce. You could have more cultural acceptance in medicine. You could have fewer hassles in a regular job, but you love expressing yourself through chiropractic, you love life, you love people and you delight in the delivery of your art.

To really shine, the Q3 part needs a procedure to follow. These are found in the Quest Procedures for Lifetime Care, (QPFLTC). These procedures take practice members on their clinical and educational journey of ascension in a tactically excellent and engaging way, consistent with a defined design. The Q3 connection and bonding part is what engages practice members in lifelong relationships that build your legacy.

You will also be aware that within each Quadrant there is another Quadrant, and in turn, these Quadrants contain further Quadrants. Each layer provides further distinctions of the primary Quadrant's function.

In every Delivery encounter you will see the 4 Quadrants being expressed, as follows.

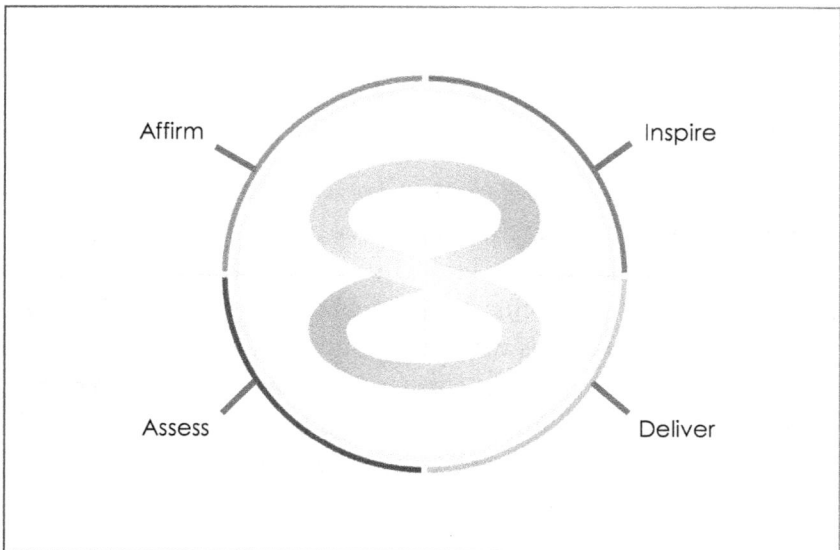

Yes, the key to Delightful Delivery in the attractive practice, with every encounter, every visit by every team member – is: *Inspire, Assess, Deliver, Affirm.*

Here's an example of how it can work;

Sally has been a colleague for a long time, and is a joy to witness in practice. Seamlessly, subtly and quite unconsciously, she demonstrates these four aspects in every visit.

The inspire aspect comes through noticing. Perhaps it's a haircut, or a new pair of shoes. She will notice and make a positive comment, an affirmation of this person's choices or their situation. She makes sure that's her first point of contact, with every person she meets.

The process of assessment is very specific and systematised. She plays a predictable role with every person. This predictability provides nurture: the person knows they are in the right place and that she knows what she is doing. They are nurtured by familiarity, certainty, and the absence of surprises. Her assessments are always thorough and polished. There is a professionality and confidence in the way she delivers her care.

This leads to the delivery – the adjustment. It is specific, explained along the way, and the delivery is communicated well as she goes. This way, the person knows what to expect. There are no surprises, even if she introduces a new adjustment.

Finally, she moves to the last stage. As the person gets up to leave, or as she leaves their presence, there is an affirmation that they will notice the difference. She will comment on their progress and tell them what to expect; in doing so, she affirms them. As she leaves, and because of her personal connection with them, she will affirm them – a hug with some, a hand on the shoulder or a high five for others. Each person leaves affirmed and uplifted by the experience.

It's no wonder that Sally has a long waiting list.

Here, in the delivery of the chiropractic experience, all four Quadrants have been touched. There is a completeness about this, but also a tacit call-back: to continue improving and ascending for the benefit of all.

The relationship between you and your practice member continues to flourish.

Playtime

- Design Delightful Delivery for every visit for your practice.

Summary

- Q3 focuses on connecting and engaging with practice members, adjusting them, and using techniques to restore optimal function.
- Connection and bonding in Q3 leads to lifelong relationships and a legacy for the chiropractor.
- The key to Delightful Delivery in the attractive practice is to Inspire, Assess, Deliver, Affirm on every encounter.

Strategy 5: Defined Design

The 8 Strategies Of The Attractive Practice Model

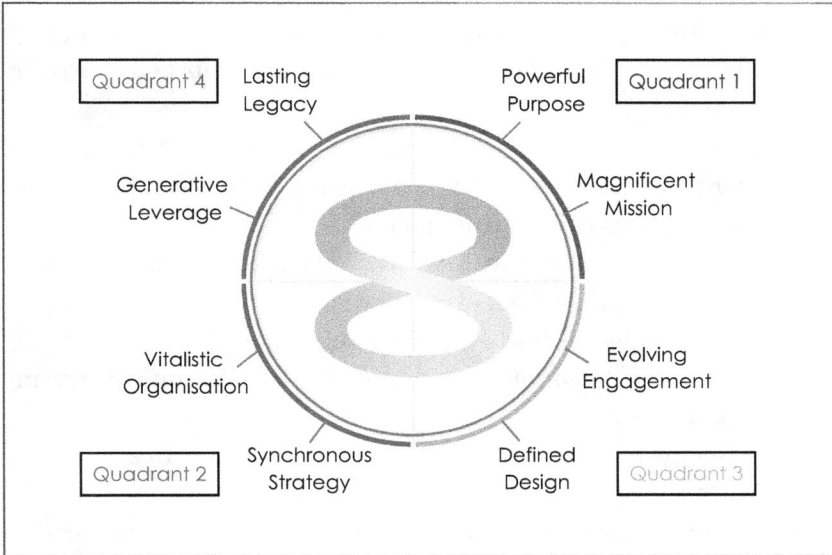

You owe it to those people who have put their trust and faith in you to have a well-defined design for each of them as a unique individual. Ask yourself, "How does our 'defined design' look, feel, and flow from one visit to the next"?

When you have clarity about your why, what and how, you will ensure that this energy carries through into the practice member's experience every time they come through your door.

People have limits to comprehending large amounts of information, so they need to have it layered in a way that makes sense to their limited understanding of your field.

You need to start with the design in mind. Consider where the person is at regarding their expectations, health care behaviours and level of philosophical awareness. (Sometimes this is tricky to read and may lead to some surprises, so don't pre-judge.)

- Know where you want to ascend this person to (the very best-case scenario) and get clear about the stages you will take them through as they gain understanding and awareness of their body, environment, and self.
- Utilise the environment you bring your people into; it's an integral component of nurture. Go into your practice after hours and take in the vibe. Five-sense the practice.
  - Crawl around on the floor – what does the carpet smell like?
  - Get under the tables – is there dust and dirt there?
  - Look at the ceilings – are there cobwebs?
  - Sit in the reception room – how are the seats, upholstery and paintwork?
  - Get the feel of what the walls are saying and notice what your kinaesthetic responses to these inputs are.
- Prioritise creating and rolling out a clear design for your services delivery.

Your team and your practice members are the most important ingredients of your business. This is where your income comes from so make sure it gets priority attention.

Playtime

- Take the time to investigate the design, look, feel, taste and touch of your premises.

Summary

- Know where you want to ascend the person to and be clear about the stages to take them through as they gain understanding and awareness.
- Have a well-defined design for each practice member as a unique individual.
- Clarity about the why, what, and how to ensure energy carries through each visit.
- Create and roll out a clear design for your services delivery.
- Layer communication in a way that makes sense to their understanding.
- Utilise the practice environment as an integral component of nurture.
- Prioritise your team and practice members as they are the most important ingredients of your business

The Right Players in the Right Places at the Right Time

You are in the people business and Delightful Delivery is a huge asset. Chiropractic's viewpoint is that every person is complete and whole and has all parts necessary to live out their destiny. You and your team are here to remove any impediments to that wholeness. The *in8model*® sees us as whole-brained beings. It sees a flow that moves across the hemispheres of the brain, engaging creativity and analysis, inspiration and strategy. These flow in a logical sequence that builds structure, leading to optimised growth and improvement.

In the Deliver section, we can appreciate the diversity that each person offers, and consciously set up the business 'brain' with the in-8model® as a guide.

To spend time and energy retraining yours or others' 'not me' part is a frustrating and energy-consuming exercise. It is more logical to hire the right person with the right attributes at the right time.

Let's look at the design of the people part of your practice team.

A Practice Team of Four Parts...

I developed the in8model® over the last 40 years, as I observed human behaviour and character preferences and compared them to others' work on the subject over the recorded history of mankind. I am sure you have noticed that we all experience the world from different perspectives.

Let's use the archetypes I described in the in8model® in the context of your practice to illustrate the differences in your team.

It's a Sunday evening, eating dinner together after a chiropractic conference. The silence is broken by the youngest and most excitable of the group; an enthusiastic girl we shall call Holistic Helen.

"That was amazing! So many things to take away from it and put into practice tomorrow! I'm so inspired! We can change the front desk around, introduce prepay, and bring all of our talks back to life..." Helen cried in her usual expressive style.

This exclamation produces a terse response from the office manager, Correct Cathy.

"Don't be so irresponsible, Helen. We can't overhaul everything by first thing tomorrow morning. We need to think this through, put some structure around it. Let's start with a planning session – we can break down the big changes we need to make, and then train up the CAs and Associates. We need our systems, policies, and procedures to reflect our new direction. We can't just go changing overnight. Plus, you did this last time you went to a conference, and the practice was an absolute shemozzle for weeks."

At the mention of introducing these changes, their associate Loyal Larry uncurls himself from his comfortable position on the couch (texting friends). "Look, I just want to be able to make things better for our people. I was listening in those technique sessions, and feeling sorry for at least a dozen of our practice members. I've been racking my brains over how I could better help them. What they talked about in the workshop is exactly what they need. How it rolls out doesn't bother me, just as long as my people get the benefit."

"Settle down," chastises Action Adam. "We need to consider the logistics of all of this. We need to put this into workable, sustainable, scalable action steps that we can rollout across the practice and really improve it. Then everything Helen is talking about will be not only achievable, but scalable. If, and that's a big if, we do it right."

His response prompts cries of "It'll be fine! Just think of the possibilities!" from Holistic Helen, while Correct Cathy states she isn't willing to risk it without adequate planning. Loyal Larry's mind is still on the practice members he's been worried over. He is writing down a list of names. Holistic Helen becomes increasingly excited at the opportunities revealed in all they learned, and begins rapidly suggesting possible themes, strategies, mentors, and more.

Meanwhile, Correct Cathy is getting increasingly frustrated as she remembers all the mistakes that were made after their last haphazard rollout. She is thinking about how to avoid any potential problems.

Loyal Larry replies that he doesn't care as long as his people get the benefit and it doesn't involve any disruption to the normal flow.

All this time, Action Adam has been crunching numbers on his phone. He announces that they need to have a conversation about how they could 10X the practice, based on the ideas that came from the conference.

And so the discussion continues. Holistic Helen vividly describes the ways they can re-engage people in their practice, and, "Oh! We could have a practice-wide launch party and invite EVERYONE!!". Correct Cathy insists they slow down and put the planning, policies, procedures and strategies in place first. Loyal Larry assures them *all that he's easy and just wants everyone to benefit from their great care provided there is no interruption to normal procedures.*

Action Adam simply retorts, "At the end of the day, it's got to be growing and revenue-positive – that's all I care about."

Whilst I have depicted the in8model® family as individual people for ease of understanding, they actually represent the parts of you and your team. These different parts, drawn from the four quadrants, are what bring power to you and your practice. You will notice when you are or are not "doing" your Holistic Helen, Correct Cathy, Loyal Larry, or Action Adam parts. Based on this observation, you may then ask the question: "How is this serving me or my practice?" The point here is that all behaviour is useful – *in a certain context.*

Selecting the appropriate resources or people to meet a given circumstance can be literally life changing. Being able to do it purposefully and with ease is a skill that, once learned, has no end of potential benefits both in personal and practice terms.

Finding the Right Team

Having the Team Centred Mission in place (which you completed in Part 1), you will have the ideal team members' profiles sorted. Have all your team do the in8model® Quiz and identify where your team's gaps are. Always hire for the gaps, both the character and the skill gaps.

It's important that your team does the hiring. Don't rely on an outside agency. You must take responsibility for this function. You know your practice's culture better than an outside agency. That way you are 90% of the way to manifesting the new team member. You will hire tens if not hundreds of team members in your practice lifetime. So, be responsible for getting good at it.

Before hitting the airwaves and advertising, check out who may be moving towards you. The perfect person may well be in your circle of influence, either within the practice now or in a place known to you.

If you advertise make sure you include the key words from the Team Centred Mission document. The person with the right character traits will resonate with these.

Remember, you are hiring primarily for character, so consider this when interviewing – make it experiential.

Playtime

- Identify the Quadrant preferences of your ideal team members in their respective roles.
- Have all your team do the in8model® Quiz.
- What are the gaps in your team?
- For the specifics of team hiring, check out our complete guide in the Hire Your Super CA program.

Summary

- Different people experience the world from different perspectives.
- When personal uniqueness is accepted, it makes everything and everyone more attractive.
- Hire for the gaps.
- Get good at hiring. You will probably do it hundreds of times in your practice life.

Onboarding and Training Your Team Members

Training a new team member is expensive. (We estimate upward of $10,000 per CA and $50,000 per Associate.) BUT the cost of *not* doing it is way more expensive, and it keeps on costing in time, money and lost opportunity. For your delivery to be delightful and for your practice to be attractive you must have exquisite team members playing together as a cohesive team.

Invest in your team *big time*. I assert that every person on this planet is a diamond in the rough. If you choose them by character trait, elements of the diamond within will be shining through. You must make a judgement call about not accepting too much 'rough' in the hope of it shining brightly under your tutelage at some time in the future – that is not your primary job. Your job is to serve humanity, not to be a home for lost dogs.

Your training should include all of the Quadrants. It runs like this:

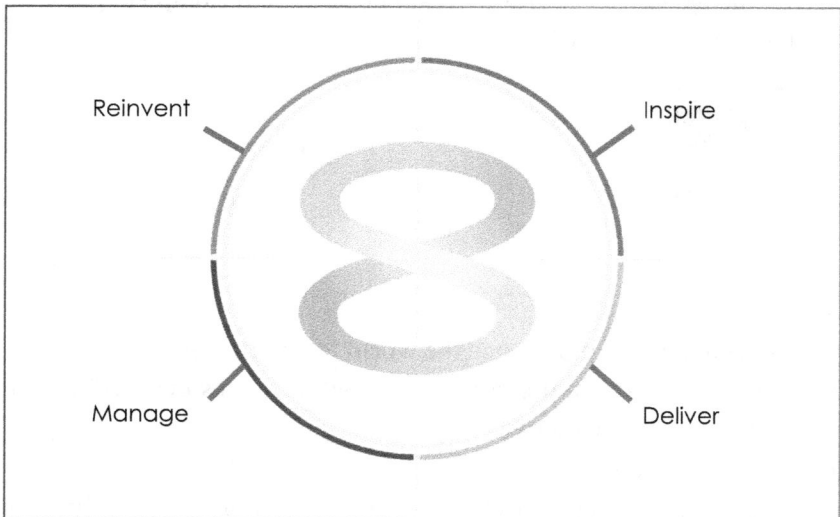

Q1 – Purpose

You want the new recruit to have a clear idea of the big why. They need to have full buy in to the purpose of this particular activity/process/thing, so they have a context for it.

Q2 – Details

Help the person understand what the activity/process/thing is. The details are where genius lies so make sure that the new team member understands the basic elements and appreciates that there are many layers beneath which they will uncover as they ascend in the practice.

Q3 – Process

Now that they understand why they would do it, what specifically it is, they will then be open to understanding and using it. The process spells out the specific steps to take in performing the task.

Q4 – Exceptions

As with every procedure there are exceptions. Some exceptions show themselves right up front and some can be quite unique to a given person or situation. Be aware that when it comes to individuals, nothing is 'one size fits all' so note the differences and the nuances. This builds a repertoire of possible options over time.

Having a mentor to follow accelerates the new recruit's learning, so make sure they shadow the right person for their intended role. If this is your first team member, ask a local practitioner you respect to have your new team member visit their practice and observe their processes for several shifts. Most chiropractors are only too happy to help, so be sure to ask.

Having a complete Office Policy and Procedures Manual (OPM) is the onboarding and training dream but don't sweat it if yours isn't complete yet. Use the new recruit to help build it by recording their observations and comparing them with either what is written in the OPM or with what should or shouldn't be going in the OPM. This speeds the new team member's understanding, corrects errors currently being made and avoids confusion in the process, completing the OPM faster.

The OPM can be a huge undertaking, as we described in the previous Section. If you want to short circuit this process, we have an Office Policy & Procedures Template that will make it a lot easier.

Ensure that you have checklists in place for every step of a process. The Q2 & 3 parts love to tick off the steps of a given task. Have an onboarding checklist for the initial process and a training checklist for each step of the way.

Make sure that you have a specific function checklist for the key functions of the practice (Opening, Start of Shift, End of Shift, End of Day, New Person, ROF, etc.).

Accountability demands that every action is signed off by the responsible team member, not just ticked. The Checklists are scrutinised by the nominated person at the end of every week.

Examples of Checklists

PLEASE INITIAL - DO NOT TICK						
Opening Procedures Checklist	**Mon**	**Tues**	**Wed**	**Thurs**	**Fri**	**Sat**
Doors, lights air con						
Front Desk computers & software						
TV & Rolling Powerpoint (Set to repeat)						
Report & Scan room computers						
X-Ray computer & printer						
Back office computer						
Safe - keys, floats, KSO satchel						
Back up tape - change						
Items for Front Desk pigeon hole						
Answer machine						
Sliding doors						
Open toilet window, close door						
Aromatherapy burner						
Water feature						
Aromatherapy oil spray						
Glasses of water for chiros						
Check shift files						
Shift pre brief						

PLEASE INITIAL - DO NOT TICK						
End of Shift Checklist	**Mon**	**Tues**	**Wed**	**Thurs**	**Fri**	**Sat**
Bins - garbage & cardboard out						
Tidy Back Office - dishes, benches						
Tidy adjusting rooms/areas						
Towels & foot stools for next shift						
Gloves and face paper						

Obviously, each of the activities on the Checklist are fully written up in the Office Policy and Procedures Manual and the relevant CAs' or Chiropractors' roles in the activity are assigned on the Organisational Storyboard.

The idea that 'people run systems and systems run businesses and every business is broken all the time' is useful; it helps to drive the search for never-ending improvement. Every living system (including your practice) is either growing or dying, so ongoing and never-ending learning, training and reinvention of systems is essential.

Playtime

- Have your onboarding checklists for every position in the practice.
- Have your allocation of roles designated in the Organisational Storyboard.
- Have all the activities specified in the Office Policy and Procedures Manual.
- Have training checklists for every position in the practice.

Summary

- Taking on a new team member is expensive.
- Not investing in your team can cost in time, money, and lost opportunities.
- Exquisite people playing together as a cohesive team are necessary for the Delightful Delivery of an attractive practice.
- Design training to include each of the quadrants (purpose, details, application, exceptions) and note individual differences and nuances.
- Having a mentor and observing other practitioners' processes can accelerate learning.
- Use a complete Office Policy and Procedures Manual (OPM) to onboard and train new team members.
- Checklists should be in place for every step of a given process, including specific checklists for key functions.
- The attitude of ongoing learning, training, and reinvention of systems is essential for never-ending improvement.

What Your CAs Want from their Chiropractor

All too often the chiropractor sees the CA as just the girl or guy at the front desk, who may answer the phones, keep an appointment book, and only do basic administration and reception jobs.

A CA can be so much more. A Super CA is a major force in driving a practice forward. An advocate for healthy lifestyle. A creator of innovative ideas. The Super CA is empowered to assist in the chiropractic journey of every person they encounter, inside and outside the practice.

You are probably getting used to the 4 areas of the in8model® in reference to how organisation is performed. We're going to go through them as they relate to your CA's needs.

What does your CA need from the Q1 part, where our purpose, beliefs, outcome, mission, and all those big picture things reside? They need to be taken on a journey, the bigger the better. Remember planning for a big trip. The excitement, anticipation and organisation were compelling. You imagined yourself seeing the sights and sensing the energy of your destination, and you felt the energy way ahead of the event. Now, compare this to the everyday chore of going to the corner shop to buy some butter – predictable and unexciting. Always keep the big picture outcome in the forefront of your CA's mind, just as you do with your practice members.

Every meeting is an opportunity to remind your team of the massive impact you are all having on people's lives.

As Chiropractors, we spend time and money learning; reading, at seminars, with coaches and with consultants, working out how to solve a particular problem, how to expand our practice, how to inspire people further, how to leverage our resources, or how to market and connect with people more effectively.

All too often we overlook the massive resource of those amazing Super CAs in our corner, chomping at the bit to help us. Many times, we don't take our CAs on our journey. They sit there passively, just waiting for the Boss to come marching in on a Monday morning after another seminar with another big new idea, which usually means more work for the CAs. There's a reluctant, "OK..." from the team, but they are actually thinking, "They'll get over this by Friday, so let's not take it too seriously."

In this scenario the CAs are lacking enough Q1 'Why'. Usually, CAs have Q2 and Q3 preferences, dealing in the practical details. But, they still need to be engaged with the concepts. Initially, their contribution to your great idea might be, "No, we have tried this in the past", or, "No, it won't work here." No matter how good it is they'll find what's wrong with it. Don't think they're throwing cold water on your ideas. It's just that people who are strong in Q2 see it as their role and responsibility to find problems with the proposal, while the Q3 part is dedicated to finding solutions to the problem; together they will work towards actualizing the vision of the Q1 part. What they're really saying is, "Well, hang on, what about this? And what about that? And have we thought about this other thing?"

Your CAs need to be participants in conceiving and constructing the journey. They need to understand the relevance to the purpose, mission and the outcomes of the practice of any new thought. They need to be involved in hashing these things out, raising problems and disagreeing, so they have ownership of the new development.

Sure, this takes longer than the old mechanistic, top-down management system driven by the person with the superior title, but this vitalistic system of innovation and implementation is highly effective, and engages the whole team in the 'why' of the journey. The more they own what you're doing, the more they will drive it with you.

So, what do your CAs need to become Super CAs?

Give them clarity around their roles, jobs and priorities. Ensure that you and your team are really clear on each other's roles and jobs, and the priorities of those jobs. Having clearly defined structure and process makes CAs feel safe and nurtured. If they don't feel safe, they will pull back and only do what they know, because the fear of being wrong is stronger than the draw of risk-taking.

Our coaching clients are constantly telling us that when their team go through the QPFLTC and the Voyage Chart™, something within them 'clicks'. (See the Journey and the Voyage charts at the beginning of the book). The job descriptions, checklists and storyboard structure give the entire team the confidence to take on new roles and move forward with enthusiasm.

The critical factors in all relationships are connection, engagement and communication. Your CAs are no exception. They need regular connection points with you. Even if you're a wonderfully kind person and you're super approachable, I can tell you now that CAs find it very hard to raise issues with their bosses.

In order to develop engagement and communication, you need regular connection points, and a culture that allows discussion about pain points, ideas and priorities.

Activities like pre- and post-shift huddles, team meetings and trainings, and of course, social events (one-on-one or with the whole team) will keep the team relationships on point and your culture will flourish.

The ultimate thing your CAs need from you is trust. People are empowered when they are trusted to make decisions, and to be accountable for them. Your CAs need to be empowered to lead a shift.

You are the practitioner, the expert in your space. Allow the CAs to be the experts in their space. If they know they actually run the shift, they will keep that appointment book flowing, keep the culture going, keep the environment optimised. Your CAs have the potential to lift to a whole new level, but they can't if you don't let them. If you keep stepping into their lane, they're forced to step back. So, empower them to run the shift and you focus on being the best you can be.

One of many examples of this are the Chiropractors who overreach their role by stepping behind the front desk. This disempowers your CAs and they are unable to operate to the best of their ability. They are best left to run the front desk (even if you could do it better), so make sure that you create a space where they can be empowered to take the lead. If you are aware of issues with the CAs, get them sorted at the appropriate time (trainings, meetings, huddles, etc.)

All right. Keep in mind that Chiropractic Assistants are assistants to ChiropracTIC, not ChiropracTORS – they're not your personal assistants. They facilitate the journey of chiropractic, the big picture of chiropractic and the moving forward of people's ascension as human beings. If you elevate them to their capacity, you will find that they take what you're doing and lift it to the next level. They're going to come up with ideas and processes that make things more effective. They're going to expand the practice.

The saying that a rising tide lifts all boats is so relevant. Empower your CAs to become Attractive Super CAs.

This is what CAs want from their Chiropractors.

Playtime

- Keep to your own lane and let your CAs keep to theirs.
- Check out our Hire Your Super CA program.
- Check out our Super CA courses.

Summary

- Your CAs are a major force in driving the practice forward.
- CAs are advocates for people's healthy lifestyles and creators of innovative ideas.
- The in8model® has 4 areas of organisation and CAs need to be across them all.
- CAs need to be reminded of the big picture outcomes and the impact that the practice is having on people's lives.
- CAs need to be engaged with the concepts and involved in hashing out new ideas and raising problems.
- The more CAs own the practice's culture, the more they will drive it, rather than just doing what they're told.

Meetings Matter

Your return on investment from team meetings, comradery and training will be one of the best returns ever. Your job as a practitioner is to work on your practice members *and* your team. The bigger your practice gets, the more you work on your team.

Foundational management techniques build success and momentum. One of these is the Team Meeting. Rather than waiting for a crisis, or focussing on problems or issues, bring people together to celebrate and recognise the excellent moments that build success. Systematically revisit your systems as a matter of process, not of urgency when things goes wrong.

Team Meetings can be seen as a 'necessary evil' that people avoid or mentally check out of, or they can be transformative. If you choose to have your practice be a transformative place, then your meetings need to be likewise.

The assortment of meetings or targeted interactions, as we prefer to see them, range from chance meetings to retreats. They could be summarised as follows:

Hallway meetings – These little meetings could be dealing with a positive or negative event or circumstance that has just happened. Many of the biggest awakenings occur for associates when a CA or senior practitioner overhears and shares opportunities for improvement at these two-minute meetings.

Daily Huddles – The pre- and post-shift huddles respectively set the scene for the shift to come and edit the shift that was. This assists in pre-framing and reframing the events to ensure that they flow well now and in the future.

Practitioner Meetings – These weekly meetings at an agreed-upon, prescribed time give the practitioners an opportunity to address content related to their interests. Having an agenda is useful, but it must be 'set in jelly', as the challenge or opportunity of the week always takes precedence.

Team Meetings – Ensure that your team commits to the meetings, which should occur regularly, at least two per month. Have the focus of one meeting on the right brain and the other on the left brain, but both should cover all Quadrants. Make sure they happen regardless of whether key people are there or not. Have a different chair every month for all scheduled meetings.

The agenda should include:

• An inspirational segment.
• Covering each Quadrant of the Operational Storyboard.
• Care Assessments being read out and appropriate actions taken.
• Clinical success stories and observations presented by each team member.

- Reciting and performing the Practice Statement Of Purpose at the end of the meeting.

Team Training – Trainings around a specific topic/policy/procedure should be scheduled regularly. Depending on the stage of the practice this may range from every week to 8-weekly.

They may be mentoring sessions with practitioners and CAs regarding topics that are relevant to each party, or they may be group trainings around skills and behaviours.

Retreats – These are immersion opportunities that bring the team together. It may be in conjunction with a seminar, but it also may be a location that stimulates physical, mental and emotional growth.

Celebrations – Plan at least two a year, where team members and their loved ones can gather and celebrate their journey together. Christmas is obviously an ideal time for a celebration for the year gone by. Maybe Christmas in July can be a good halfway marker. We decide on a surprise element for our Christmas event, and it involves significant anticipation and 'left field' experiences.

Playtime

- Organise your Meeting Agenda.
- Make sure that your meetings are scheduled appropriately.
- Get your retreats and celebrations planned and booked.

Summary

- Investing in team meetings, comradery, and training provides excellent returns.
- Practitioners should work on their practice members and their team to build success and momentum.

- Foundational management techniques, such as team meetings, are essential for success.
- Team meetings should celebrate successes and systematically re-visit systems.
- Team meetings can be transformative and should cover all operational quadrants.
- Other targeted interactions include hallway meetings, daily huddles, practitioner meetings, team training, retreats, and celebrations.
- The agenda for team meetings should include an inspirational segment, covering all quadrants of the operational storyboard, care assessments, clinical success stories, and reciting the Practice Statement Of Purpose.
- Regular team training should be scheduled for specific topics along with policies, procedures, scripts and variations.
- Retreats provide opportunities for team immersion and growth.
- Celebrations should be held at least twice a year.

Excellence

Simon was just getting underway with our coaching program and he had a litany of issues. He was frustrated and irritated with the team members. Practice members were bringing a laundry list of problems every visit. Too many practice members were missing appointments. Numbers were down. Referrals were down. Things were not what Simon desired or designed.

Whilst there are a million approaches to addressing these problems, we went for a simple little process. We resorted to a tool that a CA had introduced into our practice many years before. We had Simon cut out a piece of soft and woolly red sheepskin in the shape of a heart. He attached it to the side of the door that led from the team room to the adjusting area.

Everyone who crossed that threshold was to gently stroke the heart and give thanks for the opportunity to serve the wonderful people of the practice, including their fellow team members. This change in state was truly transformational. Kapow! His issues were dissolved.

Your state of being defines the quality of your actions. Your state is a combination of your physiology and your internal dialogue. When they are both in alignment with your intended outcome, your behaviours are congruent with your intent and you produce a high state of excellence. This leads to a high likelihood of optimal results.

So, the state of excellence is something you do, not something you have. It's not the result that is excellent, it's the state you are in as you work towards the result that is excellent.

A state of excellence, then, is what you want your entire team and practice members to be in at all times, regardless of their individual situations or skills. Just as you hire for character, you will also identify the character traits of excellence in your practice members. Play to these in your clinical process, according to the defined design that you have for them.

Tactics

This part is about doing the right things right, at the right time. It is the expression of ethics, where we make sure that we live according to our values.

Tactics are a subset of strategy. Strategy you plan, but tactics you have up your sleeve and use as the situation presents. Tactics are how your practice's core values are expressed in a given circumstance.

As I mentioned earlier, Walt Disney was a great proponent of management by values. One day Walt, with his young nephew, was visiting Griffith Park, an amusement park in Los Angeles. The boy was excited about the upcoming experience, only to be disappointed when the horse he chose on the carousel was out of order and didn't go up and down like the others. His cotton candy (Fairy floss) was limp and soggy, not fresh and light. Then, Walt sat on a bench and snagged his pants on some chipped paint.

The experiences of this day led Walt Disney to commit to creating an amusement park where the carousel horses always went up and down, the cotton candy was fresh and crisp, and the park benches were smooth and freshly painted.

These core values drove the standard of excellence which has attracted huge crowds to Disneyland and Disneyworld. They have brought joy to the hearts of untold numbers of children worldwide, and have created a business success story beyond comprehension. In the same way, the core values we discussed in Section 1 are critical to the Attractiveness of your practice and its draw on the public.

For example, we have a core value that "every moment with us is a *WOW* moment." From the time a person phones, to when they are greeted on arrival, to their few minutes soaking up the environment of the reception area, to receiving their check and adjustment and being bid farewell as they depart – every moment should be a *WOW* moment. No matter what the circumstances, our intent is to make every moment the person is with us a *WOW* moment.

Tactics harness the values of Attract and the order of Nurture, and apply them to Deliver. Tactics are focused on the detail and flow of every instant, and are always tracking on Plan B or even Plan C.

Do you have tactics for every occasion? For example: when you have someone who is finishing up a care plan, do you have tactics to level them up to the next care plan? What about care for different stages of life, from infancy to elderly or frail care? What about the myriad of situations that people find themselves in – accidents, injuries, calamities, misfortune etc?

We all like to be acknowledged. For many, receiving an old-school, hand-printed birthday card for a significant birthday is a very special event. A random text, email or note, checking in to see how they are tracking, can be a *WOW* moment. "Random acts of kindness" comes to mind with this element of Nurture.

How about when someone is falling off their schedule? Do you have tactics to connect and re-engage, or to recognise hardship and remove the burden of guilt? Tactics cover everything from staffing, development, marketing and communication, through to the delivery of the adjustment.

The greater the repertoire of tactics, the more efficient and effective your delivery will be.

Playtime

- Review your Operational Core Values.
- Make sure that your Core Values are being expressed in your day to day tactical delivery.
- Make sure that your team is acutely aware of these tactics.

Summary

- Tactics are a subset of strategy.
- Core Values are expressed through tactics.
- Walt Disney's commitment to Core Values led to the success of Disneyland and Disneyworld.
- Core Values are critical to the attractiveness of a practice.
- Tactics focus on the details and flow of every moment.

- Tactics should have a plan B or even plan C.
- Acknowledgment creates WOW moments.

How Attractive Are Your Words?

Yes, I know I mentioned it earlier, and I'm going to bang on about it again.

I've mused a lot over the years about the power of words. And why wouldn't I? I'm a chiropractor! Words have been a big point of difference for us, and indeed, a point of contention. To me, it's always been worth the extra care and attention. Why?

Every profession has its own lexicon, based on its philosophy, science, art, and politics. When you take the lexicon from one profession (say Medicine) and apply it to another profession (say Chiropractic), you become filled with contradictions because of the dissonance between the words you use and what you do.

The alternative is to use the words that are relevant to the Chiropractic lexicon, as we will now investigate.

Words matter and in fact words *make* matter. They might be just non-sensical syllables that we string together and imbue with meaning, but that *is* the important thing. They can connect profoundly or leave your practice member lost in translation. They can empower and intrigue, or limit and confuse. Your words define your reality. So, choose your words wisely.

In 1971, Albert Mehrabian undertook research into non-verbal communication. His findings include the famous adage that only 7% of communication is verbal. The rest is tone and body language. While I'm sure another look at communication in the digital era would yield different percentages, the fact still remains that the words we communicate with are critical to our outcomes.

Words have a vibration, a representation, and a connotation. That is, there is a physical resonance about them, they represent the energy of our intended communication, and they elicit connotations in the minds of the people we are speaking with. Language changes and evolves over time. The connotation that goes with a word often shifts from its original meaning. Thus, we ought to be very careful and intentional in the way we deliver messages and meanings via the medium of speech.

Let's check a few commonly used words that we've adopted in Chiropractic.

How about **patient**? Something you'll likely have noticed is that I don't refer to practice members as **patients**. This was a deliberate decision because of the meaning that is so deeply associated with the word **patient.**

The last time I checked, the Oxford Dictionary defines **patient** as "A person receiving medical treatment." Sure, you will attend to people who need treatment, but if they choose to go beyond that and optimise their health, that label and its associated attitude no longer fits.

If you refer to your practice members as **patients**, you will limit their experience. The classic oxymoron is 'the wellness patient!'

In contrast, the dictionary says that a **person** is 'A human being regarded as an individual'. Using this word frees you up to marvel at the uniqueness and attractiveness of the individual.

I went to the Oxford Dictionary for the English meaning of some other commonly used words germane to our profession.

How about **symptoms**? "A physical or mental feature which is regarded as indicating a condition of disease." Or, there are **signs**: "An object, quality, or event whose presence or occurrence indicates the probable presence or occurrence of something else". This opens you up to explore the greater dynamics of the whole person.

Then, **treatment**? "Medical care given to a patient for an illness or injury." How about **care**? "The provision of what is necessary for the health, welfare, maintenance and protection of someone or something". What an attractive scope.

There is **convert**: "Change one's religious faith or other belief." How about **nurture**? "Care for and protect (someone or something) while they are growing." This speaks to accepting others as they are and respecting the differences.

Then there is **retention**: "The continued possession, use, or control of something." How about **ascension**? "The action of rising to an important position or a higher level." Rather than holding on or holding back, we can all grow together.

There is **paediatrics**: "The branch of medicine dealing with children and their diseases." Or there is simply chiropractic care for **children**: "Young children below the age of puberty." You nurture them to ascend and optimise.

Then there is the word **clinic**. This is described as "An establishment or hospital department where outpatients are given medical treatment or advice, especially of a specialist nature." Or there is **practice**: "The carrying out or exercise of a profession."

If you are intent on ascending yourself and your practice members as you share this journey together, make sure you use the appropriate words to maximise the potential in both your practice and your people.

Playtime

- Note the areas where you can clean up your words.
- Hold each other accountable for your agreed word usage. (Remember that they determine your reality and your future).

Summary

- Words have power and can impact your outcomes.
- The words we use define our reality and can connect or confuse.
- Every profession has its own lexicon, based on its philosophy, science, art, and politics.
- When you take the lexicon from one profession (say Medicine) and apply it to another profession (say Chiropractic), you become filled with contradictions.
- The alternative is to use the words that are relevant to the Chiropractic lexicon.

Technique

Your choice of technique is something you have decided, after researching and educating yourself, is the best choice. To this, I would add, "so far". Everything, including our professional body of knowledge, is growing and changing, and you never know what technique may have your name on it down the track.

Technique comes after you have done the work of the Q1 Why and the Q2 What. The question then is the Q3 How. HOW do I apply my ideas so that my walk is aligned with my talk?

The technique that you use is a big part of your brand. It defines your unique, attractive practice. So, decide with care, and remember, it takes 10,000 hours to become accomplished at any skill, so practice, practice, practice.

If you want to leverage your practice to include other practitioners, then choose a technique which is taught and certified by an outside party so you will have consistency of quality. Many chiropractors create a noose for their own necks by making up their own techniques which no one can duplicate, and they are left without the ability to take time off or scale the business.

The Delivery of your offering is based upon the 4 factors of technical excellence as follows:

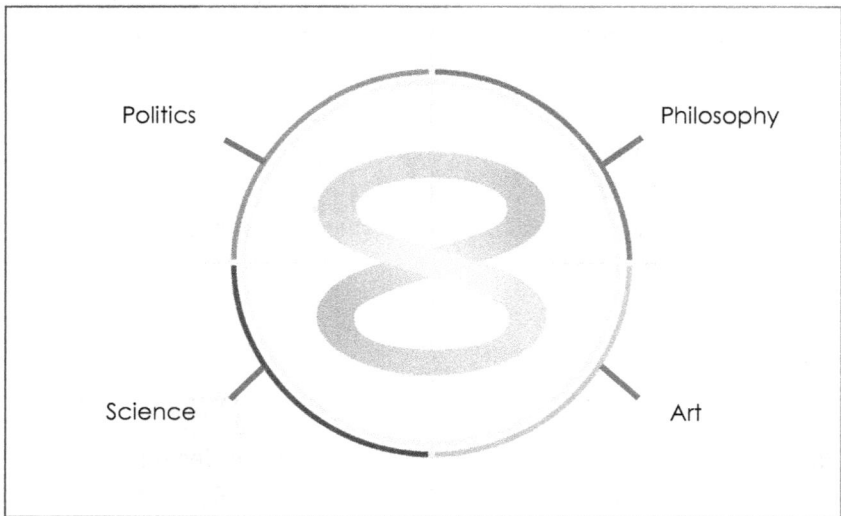

Q1 – Philosophy

Your Philosophical viewpoint (Q1) is based upon values and beliefs. Is it vitalistic or mechanistic?

Q2 – Science

This viewpoint then feeds into your scientific paradigm (Q2). Is it a segmented or synchronous model?

Q3 – Art

The application of your art (Q3) follows. What is your optimal outcome for your people, and is there a clear protocol for assessing, adjusting and reassessing?

Q4 – Politics

From the application (Q3), you will proliferate and expand your viewpoint (Q4). This is your narrative – your story. It may be increasing your service through associates or multiple practices, teaching your technique, or serving in some other capacity to expand the technique that is close to your heart. Is the technique duplicable, so others can produce the same results from the same indicators?

Your task is to produce predictable results in a state of excellence.

Above your intent, your knowledge and your technical ability is the essence of you. This is your present time consciousness. This is you being you and being one with the person you are serving right now. You are being Attractive when your delivery of your professional services causes people to say WOW. Every time you impart information and knowledge it truly shifts people's reality. Every time you empower people to appreciate their own innate wisdom they move to a better version of themselves.

Your technical elegance attracts more people towards you. Those people will come back to you because of how they feel when they are with you. They will pay whatever the cost, travel whatever the distance, and refer their friends to you by the bus load.

Playtime

- Rate yourself on your 4 Factors of Technical Excellence.

- Be constantly aware of your present time consciousness.
- Develop a plan to increase your score in each area.

Summary

- Your technique is your chosen vehicle for carrying out your defined design for your client's ascension.
- Technique comes after figuring out the Why and the What of your practice.
- The technique you use is part of the unique, attractive design of your practice.
- Choose a technique that is taught and certified by an outside party for consistency of quality.
- Your task is to produce consistent and predictable results in a state of excellence, elegance and ease.

Care Scheduling

Schedules of care can be one of the most confusing and controversial components of practice delivery. Many chiropractors are unsure about the best approach to provide the optimal outcomes for their practice members without over or under servicing. There are many facets and individual considerations to this topic. Not getting it right can lead to frustration and poor outcomes for everyone – especially your practice members.

Let's consider the practice member's journey. Most people, including many Chiropractors, don't take a meta-view of their life and health, so they can be forgiven for thinking that life is a series of unrelated incidents. In this context, every healthcare event is seen as a transaction, a payment in exchange for fixing a problem. How long it is going to take is directly related to how long it has been a problem. If it happened yesterday, it should be gone tomorrow. If it happened with a little movement, it should go with a little movement. I'm sure you have seen lots of these.

Chiropractors who take a meta-view of life and health create life-long relationships with their people rather than short-term Chiropractic transactions.

When you pre-frame the reason for being in the practice using the Journey model, the person understands that their position today is the result of the sum total of where they have been in their life's journey so far. The Journey model provides the opportunity to redefine their expectations of how long and how much care is required. The Journey Poster (below) is a key reference tool for demonstrating the duration of care. The metaphorical stages of Relief, Stabilisation, Regeneration and Optimisation are necessary reference markers.

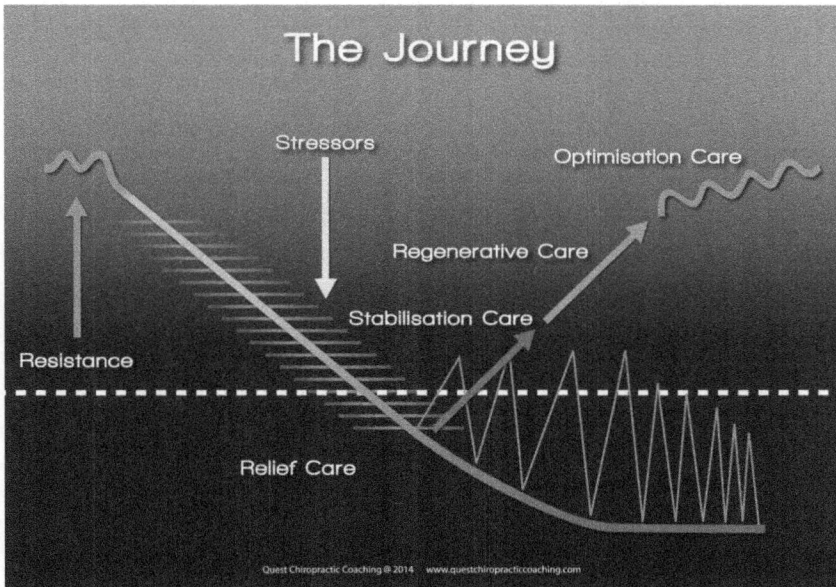

The Journey

Stressors

Optimisation Care

Regenerative Care

Stabilisation Care

Resistance

Relief Care

Quest Chiropractic Coaching © 2014   www.questchiropracticcoaching.com

When deciding on schedules of care look at the 8 Strategies that drive your practice. Each one of these strategies, as covered in this book, must incorporate your individual practice's values, beliefs and behaviours. You must decide, in order, what your philosophical viewpoints around your care are: what your mission is, why you are doing what you do, what form of organisation you will employ, what your strategies for the application will be, how you will design your delivery, how you and your team engage with your practice members, what you can do to get leverage and grow, and how everybody associated with your practice will be empowered.

When you have designed this process, you will have a well-formed structure for facilitating the clinical journey of your practice members which, along with their individual beliefs and outcomes, plus their clinical presentation, will determine the technique protocols, frequency and duration of care that you recommend.

As with every empirical science, you are working with a hypothesis. You will continually test, measure, and change your application, as you do in every relationship that you have.

Dr James L. Chestnut, in his book, 'The 14 Foundational Premises for The Scientific And Philosophical Validation Of The Chiropractic Paradigm', states that, "The chiropractic adjustment restores healthy joint biomechanics by breaking up connective tissue adhesions (scar tissue), and restores/creates healthy neurological pathways (segmental and global) by stimulating mechanoreceptors. These processes require substantial repetition through the physiological stages of healing and neuroplasticity and synaptogenesis if long term functional correction is to take place."

The physiological stages of healing that Chestnut refers to were proposed many years earlier by Troyanovich et al. in 'Structural rehabilitation of the spine and posture: Rationale for care beyond resolution of symptoms.' (JMPT, 1998).

They define three Physiological Stages of Healing, as follows:

- Acute inflammatory stage (up to 72 hours).
- Repair stage (72 hours to 6 weeks) – Random deposition of collagen (scar tissue).
- Remodeling stage (3 weeks to 12 months) – Scar tissue reoriented to increase functional capabilities (tensile strength).

If increasing neuroplasticity and remodeling soft and hard tissues is part of your agenda, then you will want to apply repetition of input over time. This requires that you give optimal recommendations for care without fear or favor. Too often a chiropractor will pre-judge a person's ability to pay or to attend and recommend too little care for the desired results. This diminishes the value of the practice or service for the practice members – it's *not* useful.

As stated previously, scheduling is a technique issue and the Journey is a metaphor, so there are no rules set in stone for the frequency and duration of care.

A typical example of an initial care schedule designed to achieve relief plus stabilisation of the presenting complaint may be full immersion of 2 or 3 times a day through to two to three times a week over 12 weeks.

Care Assessment

A subjective 'Care Assessment' to gauge the person's progress must be done halfway through the Stabilisation Care program. (For example, on the 12th visit in a 24 visit schedule.)

This will give you a heads up about the person's current perception of care. This enables you to make any necessary alterations to your application of care in the remaining half of their initial care.

Playtime

- Get clear on your care scheduling considering all criteria.
- Make sure that you do a Care Assessment halfway through Stabilisation Care. You'll find this in the Journey Resource Pack.

Summary

- Schedules of care can be confusing and controversial.
- Consider the practice member's journey.
- Healthcare events are not isolated incidents.
- The Journey Poster provides a reference tool to demonstrate the necessity for the proposed duration of care.
- When deciding on schedules of care, look at the 8 Strategies that drive practices.
- The technique protocols, frequency, and duration of care should be determined by the person's beliefs and desired outcomes, clinical presentation, and the practitioner's competence.
- Repetition over time is required for increasing neuroplasticity and remodeling of soft and hard tissues.
- Give optimal recommendations for care without bias.
- Make sure that you perform a Care Assessment halfway through Stabilisation Care.

Progressive Exams and Reports

The progressive exam and report complete a phase of care and open up the next phase of the person's journey. Whilst every visit is a WOW visit, remember to *always* have people looking forward to their next care event, be it an exam, scan, x-ray, review, assessment, milestone, achievement, progressive exam, report or reassessment, etc.

When people run out of a future with you, they will run out the door, so make sure they are progressing toward the next big thing. The Attractive Practice Model is based upon management by agreement, so ensure that you have a strong agreement with every practice member. If that agreement is not honoured by the practice member, it is your role to make a new agreement with them.

If Regenerative Care is subsequently chosen, then the cycle of two times per week for 12 weeks, for maybe a number of years, may be indicated. However, the duration of each cycle should always be restricted, and 12 weeks is reasonable in this context.

The progressive exams and reports plus the practice member's outcomes determine the care schedule on an ongoing basis.

Frequency and duration for Optimisation Care is determined by the practice member's history, state of being, lifestyle, allostatic load and, of course, their desired outcomes and objectives. Optimisation care implies a lifelong relationship, but, as with everything in life, many circumstances can alter this.

Membership of the Healthy Lifestyles Club formalises this phase of care. The HLC program provides additional benefits to loyal practice members. Quest clients use an agreement, renewed annually, or sooner if needed.

Playtime

- Have your Progressive Exams and Reports well defined and scheduled for every practice member.
- Consider whether a Healthy Lifestyles Club is right for your practice.

Summary

- Progressive exams and reports mark the completion of a phase of care and lead to the next phase of the journey.
- It is important to keep people looking forward to the next stage of care.
- The Attractive Practice Model is based on management by agreement, so agreements must be made and honored.
- If Regenerative care is elected, it may involve two times per week for 12-week cycles.
- Progressive exams determine the care schedule.
- Optimization Care is determined by the practice member's lifestyle, including their history, state of being, allostatic load, desired outcomes and objectives.
- Healthy Lifestyles Club membership formalises this phase of care and offers additional benefits to loyal practice members.

Communicating Schedules to Practice Members

Models, analogies, and metaphors, objective tests and criteria, and the subjective Quality of Life measurements are effective ways for people to understand the necessity for care beyond relief. It is sometimes a challenge for practice members to understand that regeneration takes time. They think that one adjustment puts the bone back in place, and that it won't need any more attention because it's 'fixed'.

Many chiropractors get frustrated by society's ignorance in these matters. A paradigm shift does not occur in a nanosecond. Change happens in baby steps. I encourage you to work as if you have a lifetime with each practice member, taking baby steps together.

A dialogue in this instance may go like this:

"Repetition over time is required to create new habits – you know when a person breaks their arm and it's in a sling for six weeks? Can they use it fully straight away when the plaster comes off?"

"No"

"Why?"

"Because the muscles haven't been used for six weeks."

"Yes, after six weeks immobilised in plaster, the brain has registered a new normal. It will take a month or so for it to regain it's original function. And that's after only six weeks. So imagine, in your case it's been 35 years since your spine stopped moving properly – what is going to have to happen now?"

"Well, it'd need repetition for quite a long time."

"Exactly. That's why we do repetition over time. We make an adjustment and your body accepts it, but then the memory system tends to go back to the old normal. Before that happens you will have your next adjustment and your body goes to the next higher level of function. It's a process of rinse and repeat. It's like school. To learn a new behaviour it takes repetition over time. We're here to teach your brain and body better ways of functioning and performing. Are you with me?"

"Yes"

The QPFLTC is a total game-changer. When your practice members understand the Journey model, they get this simple and sensible message: it took time to arrive at where they are now, and it will take time to get where they want to be.

Call on your wonderful supply of simple analogies and metaphors to explain the importance of repatterning the neurological pathways. Use examples that the person will relate to. These are far more effective than long lectures around Wolf's law or the Piezoelectric effect, for example.

Using this approach, your practice will shift to a place where people stay, pay and refer their friends and family for a lifetime. because they understand WHY, in their language, they are engaging with you as they do.

Playtime

- Ensure that you have a workable model that communicates their journey to your people.
- Use metaphors, stories and analogies that people can relate to.
- Summary
- Models, analogies, stories and metaphors are more effective than lectures on technical subjects.
- Repetition over time is required to create new habits and patterns of bodily function.

Strategy 6: Evolving Engagement

The 8 Strategies Of The Attractive Practice Model

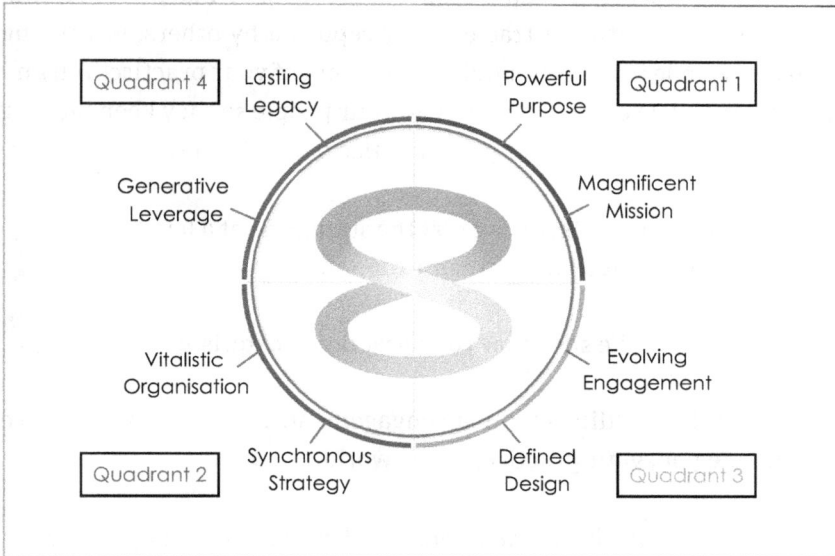

If your objective is to assist your practice members to ascend, to evolve, to transcend their previous best, then you understand that the most important moment with your people is right now. The most powerful state is one of full engagement, a state of being one with the person, where they are at, for the short time you are with them. Every visit is a continuation of a conversation. People's perception of value and connection has less to do with time spent and more to do with intimacy, proximity, tactile engagement and a shared reality.

This builds legendary attractive practices, generational in their effect.

You and your practice are in the people business. You are a living system, continuously either growing or dying, evolving or devolv-

ing. Whether your practice is evolving or devolving depends on the exquisiteness of your engagement with your practice members.

This is the attractive factor.

You and your practice members are not robots or machines. All human beings are either attracted to or repulsed by others, to varying degrees. People are either moving into or out of your practice. You and your team must remain attractive to your people so they keep moving towards you. The success of your practice depends on this.

Your ethical responsibility is to set the standards at a level that everyone can aspire to. It's big. It's inspirational.

Your role is to make sure that your practice is exquisite.

You do this by building exquisite engagement. You never know where it will take you, your practice, or the world.

Emma was just a kid when we first met her. She would come in each week to get adjusted with her parents, and it was always a delight to see her. As the years went on she became the typical teenager. Everything was about her. During this time, she attracted some interesting people and situations into her sphere.

After many adventures, she decided to go to chiropractic college. The journey was profound. Emma was motivated to serve humanity through chiropractic. I have no idea of her academic transcript from college – all I know is what I saw in practice. Her clinical results were excellent and her connection with people was amazing. She emanated an energy that truly attracted. She was always in the moment, focused on serving the person in front of her and getting the best results for them. Gone was the girl who was the sun in her own solar system, expecting every-

thing to revolve around her. Here was a young woman who daily manifested a deep intent to serve humanity by serving individuals, one at a time.

And she did. Hundreds of them every day.

Her selfless acts of service saw practice members and money flow to her, not because she needed it but because she was operating out of her abundance. Having paid off her student loans within 18 months and saved up significant funds, she's been travelling the world for the last two years. Even in a time of severe travel restrictions, Emma has had doors open to her which many would have said were impossible. As a humble and beautiful servant of humanity, she has attracted the people, places, events and situations that many wish for all their lives.

Just this week my notifications went off, with clients and friends sending photos, videos and OMG comments from the largest chiropractic gathering in Europe. Emma received the loudest and longest standing ovation for a speaker on a stage that I have ever heard.

Now, a few short years out of chiropractic college, she is sharing her message of hope and empowerment to the profession and humanity. The ripples of impact from Emma's contribution are profound. It has and will change lives for the better, far beyond the measurable.

An attractive practice is not built by working within the classic model of competition and upselling. It is built through genuine engagement and partnership, based on a big and selfless vision. As Emma has demonstrated, being exquisite is a tangible force which has a profound impact on your life, your bank account, your community and your world.

Communication

Communication is a lifetime study, and I suggest that you dedicate significant energy and resources to it. Now, here's a statement that will need qualifying:

Great chiropractors are great communicators.

Firstly, a great talker is not necessarily a great communicator. Often it is the opposite case. Some of the most amazing chiropractors I have known can barely string two words together, but their essence oozes from them and their hands tell stories of love and compassion that see people transform in their presence.

You have your own superpowers, which you discovered in the preferences of the in8model®. Make sure you get good at using them to communicate, while respecting others' preferences.

Knowing how to read people and speak with them in their model of the world is a great skill to have.

Much of our time with coaching clients is spent on the finer details of communication.

Tweaking words, tone, tempo, pitch, physiology and a myriad other communication phenomena will cause a disproportional change in results.

Remember that great communication is in how the message is received, not how it is delivered.

Communication is measured by the response you get. If your communication meets a receptive terminal in a person's neurology, they will make meaning that resonates with them (positively or negatively), and they will respond with the feelings and actions that correspond to their interpretation, not yours.

So continue to get great at how human beings communicate, both verbally and non-verbally, with the first priority being yourself.

Knowing yourself is the beginning of all wisdom – Socrates

This book provides a formal structure of the chiropractic educational journey, but please, for all of your relationships, continue to develop yourself as an exquisite communicator.

The most important aspect of the topic of communication is that you can not NOT communicate. As we have stated, everything you say is communication, and likewise, everything you don't say is communication. Every aspect of your physical practice is a communication portal. People are constantly making meaning of each detail and fitting it into their model of the world. This builds or erodes trust and attractiveness.

Remember that *You Can NOT, NOT communicate.*

Playtime

- Commit to knowing yourself.
- Constantly learn interpersonal communication skills. (CLUE: the learning never ends.)
- Make sure that your practice is communicating your message, as described in your Core Values and Statement of Purpose.
- Get the in8model® book and develop your ability to communicate across the Quadrants.

Summary

- Communication is a crucial aspect of being a great chiropractor.

- Being a great talker does not necessarily make one a great communicator.
- Everyone has their own unique superpower in communication.
- Knowing how to read people and speak with them in their model of the world is an important skill to have.
- Fine-tuning communication can lead to a significant increase in results.
- Communication is measured in the response received, not in the delivery.
- The most important aspect of communication is that everything that is said or not said is a form of communication.
- People are constantly making meaning of every aspect of the practice. This either builds or erodes trust.
- The in8model® is a great vehicle to broaden your communication skills and abilities.

Transformation – Visit by Visit

In an earnest endeavour to serve, many Chiropractors have a tendency to over-service in the area of education, whilst under-serving in the therapeutic application. How often have you found yourself going into lecture mode with your practice members? Giving them too much information in one hit? Giving it as though this is the last time you are going to be able to enlighten them?

This is not a transformative path. Instead, leave something for next time! It is more useful to give your people something to ponder, something that interrupts their patterns of thinking, something that causes them to see things differently, something that makes them ask better questions, something with less content and more context.

No matter how informed and intelligent the practice member is, they are most likely coming from a different world to yours, even if they've been under long-term chiropractic care somewhere else. This requires a 'drip feed' approach to education. It is a process of evolving engagement and life-long learning, so don't try and fill the head of a toddler with a PhD syllabus.

There is a certain sequence of generic information that all practice members must understand and integrate into their life in order to ascend in the chiropractic context. However, the educational rhythm must be tailored to the individual's reality. Every practice member will respond to their own educational rhythm on a visit-by-visit basis. It isn't standardised. It recognises that the person under care has unique values, situations and concerns. The same information will be delivered in a variety of ways based on the person's interests and vocation. A mechanic, a lawyer, a new mum, or a soccer player would all have the same content applies with a different communication strategy. When we settle into the person's educational rhythm, we can deliver a WOW moment that hits the spot and meets them where they are at, *every single time*.

This is perhaps one of the most profound aspects of the practice journey. The process is done *with* them, rather than done *to* or *for* them. We increase their awareness little by little from visit to visit. As greater clarity and alignment are reached, consciousness and awareness will increase.

After a while, it's not so much an educational rhythm – it's a transformational rhythm.

Owning The Real Estate in Their Mind

For your practice to remain relevant and attractive over time, you must own some real estate in their mind. Whilst you only have a small fraction of the practice members' time every week, you can have their attention every waking hour of their day. The question here is, "How?"

You will know certain activities to help people if applied between visits. When they are done repeatedly over time, there is a double whammy effect. Firstly, the activity benefits the person's physical state. And secondly, it provides a constant reminder of you and your practice.

This is the real estate that we speak of.

Think of some of the things they do every day and look at how you link your presence to their activity every time they do it.

For example: they breathe, they sit, they sleep and they stand in varying proportions every day. So, if they are already doing these things then why not anchor them to you and Chiropractic so they are thinking of you as they are doing them? Show them tasks to do in each of these categories.

The more they do the tasks, the more they think of you, and the more they are attracted to your practice and chiropractic.

Playtime

- Reference your Client Centred Mission and decide on the individual educational pathway each person would need to travel.
- Outline the specific steps that you will take, visit by visit, to get your practice members to where you want them to be.
- Sort out the four brain real estate activities for the quadrant preferences of each person.

Summary

- Chiropractors tend to overeducate their people, overwhelming them with too much information at one time.
- Leave something for next time and provide something to ponder.
- Interrupt people's patterns of thinking. This makes them ask better questions.

- The educational rhythm should be tailored to the individual's reality and respond to their unique values, situations, and concerns.
- Increase people's awareness and consciousness gradually, to produce a transformational rhythm.
- Aim to own some real estate in your people's minds by anchoring their everyday activities to you.

Every Visit is an ADIO Visit

Many practitioners put huge attention on the first few visits. The thrill of the chase and the consuming of the catch seem to be the focus of attention. They go into convert mode, aiming to win the new person over to buy their way of thinking. The red carpet gets rolled out and the first month of visits are filled with all the knowledge, wisdom, and attention.

When the honeymoon is over, these special visits are replaced with regular or standard visits, and the focus goes back to pursuing another catch.

If you know that people are coming into your world for a lifetime, then the urgency to impress and the necessity to convert are diminished. There is plenty of time to develop relationships. There are plenty of opportunities to assist people to take on new thoughts and behaviours, developing their world view.

Therefore, every moment with a practice member is a moment to enjoy, educate, engage and evolve.

Every touchpoint with your practice members is an opportunity for a lightbulb moment. A time to wonder, to learn, to appreciate and to imagine what else is possible. Every time someone walks out of your practice they feel changed for the better and you feel grateful to have served. Something transformational has happened.

As we take this voyage of exploration through the Attractive Practice Model, the key theme is that, just like life flows from Above, Down and Inside, Out (ADIO), so do your connections with your practice members.

The ADIO structure is the structure of the flow of brain activity as outlined earlier. We process and understand our world through Quadrants 1-4 in that order when we are evolving and in the reverse when we are devolving.

An exquisite visit involves the 4 steps of the in8model® in sequence, as follows:

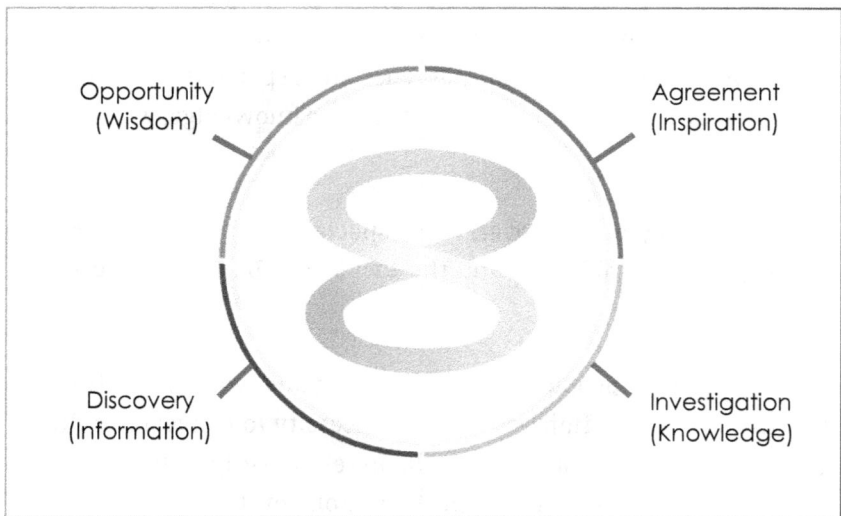

Opportunity (Wisdom)

Agreement (Inspiration)

Discovery (Information)

Investigation (Knowledge)

Q1 – Agreement

Make sure that you and your practice members are on the same page and keep your agreements. (See the Agreement frame in the 1st visit.) Meet them where they are at. Establish rapport. Go to their tonal level. Match their reality. Breathe with them.

Q2 – Discovery

What have they noticed since last time? What awareness has emerged? What realisations have they had? What connections have they made? These all add to the richness of their experience and give relevance and more attraction to their journey with you. You want them to be more informed and knowledgeable than when they arrived.

Q3. – Investigation

Engage with curiosity and investigate the amazingness of their innate wisdom. Apply your knowledge and skills in an exemplary and attractive fashion. Bring the small things to their awareness. Ask great questions that open loops. (Remember, you don't have to close them today.) Show the interconnectivity between all parts. You want them to experience the whole through a little bit of knowledge and lots of understanding.

Q4. – Opportunity

For the practice member to ascend they must expand their horizons. Send them on their way from every visit with a blessing. Always find something to empower the person with. A vision of the future. A word of hope. A ray of sunshine that brightens their day. You want them to be Wise – able to see things from a bigger perspective.

Playtime

• Incorporate the Exquisite Visit model into every visit.

Summary

- Chiropractors often focus too much on the first few visits, trying to impress and "convert" new clients to their way of thinking.
- If you see your involvement with clients as long-term, you can take more time to develop relationships and help clients evolve.
- Aim to enjoy, educate, engage, and evolve with each client at every touchpoint.
- Follow the in8model® at each visit:
  - Q1: Agreement – establish basic details and rapport, and meet people where they're at.
  - Q2: Discovery – ask about new awareness and realisations since last visit.
  - Q3: Investigation – engage with curiosity and apply curiosity, knowledge and technical skills in an exemplary and attractive fashion.
  - Q4: Opportunity – empower people with a vision of the future or a word of hope, so they can expand their horizons and see things from a bigger perspective.

Your Promise To Our People

Ultimately, the practical, delivery-focused aspect of expansion comes down to this: What is your promise to your people, *and* are you delivering on it?

This promise isn't as simple as just delivering a great adjustment and educating your people well. The promise is encapsulated in the journey you go on together. It may be a random reason, a sustainable season, or a lifetime legacy.

It doesn't have to be long and elaborate and it doesn't have to be openly shared with your practice members. They will pick up on it when you truly own it.

It may read something like this:

"We lovingly support and challenge you to experience continuous transformational shifts in your health and in your life."

OR

"Every moment with us will be a WOW moment."

OR

"We are here to remind you how great you are."

Visualise yourself looking into a practice member's eyes and letting them know that you are committed to this promise.

Playtime

- Construct your Promise To Our People statement.
- Go to your Statement of Purpose and use the key elements in all your interaction with your clients.

Summary

- Expansion is about delivering on your promise to your people.
- The promise is not just about delivering great adjustments and education, but the journey you go on together.
- The promise can be expressed in a random reason, a sustainable season, or a lifetime legacy.
- The promise doesn't have to be long or shared openly with practice members. They will pick up on it when you truly own it.

Departing is Not Loss

Whilst you know that your care is extremely valuable to your practice members, they may not have the same knowledge or appreciation as you. As stated before, people are with you for a reason, a season or a lifetime, and it's important to respect this.

People will drop out of your practice, despite your best efforts at bilateral agreement. Do your very best to make sure that all agreements are maintained. If a practice member has broken an agreement it is your job to make a new one. Even if it is driven by you and the practice member hasn't engaged, you must clean it up so the practice member doesn't carry guilt going forward.

Close Case Letters that Keep the Door Open

When people break an agreement (over, maybe, frequency and duration of care) without setting up a new agreement, the relationship can sour, leading to distancing and the corresponding justification for their actions. When a person feels this way, they will go out of their way to avoid you. They are unlikely to use your services again, let alone refer their friends to you.

This doesn't have to be. Keep your agreements clean – this is where the Close Case Letters are useful.

We have several letters that are used to close off cases. All of them have something in common:

- Acknowledgement of the fact that the situation has changed since our first agreement.
- Respect for their decision.
- Assurance of an open door and an open environment if and when they choose to re-engage.

Earlier in this book, I remarked that what we are really trading in is trust. Many practitioners choose to ignore things like Close Case Letters or Write-Off Letters (which we will cover next), but they do so at their peril. It all comes back to the trust factor. When you communicate well, you build trust. When you hold up your end of the deal, you build trust. But trust must be reciprocal. That's why when someone chooses to not complete a care plan, you respectfully acknowledge it.

You are not selling your care. You are partnering in a life journey with a person and this journey ebbs and flows. People grow and develop in surges, and they may be drawn to you at certain phases of this growth, so remain attractive to them and leave the door open with warm, friendly communication that acknowledges this.

Playtime

- Create a series of Close Case Letters that empower and bless people as they leave your practice.

Summary

- It's important to maintain all agreements, even if a practice member breaks them.
- Keep agreements clean by using Close Case Letters to maintain an open door for re-engagement.
- Trust is what you are trading in the relationship and communication builds trust.

Write-Off Letters that Clear the Waters

It's a rare chiropractor who hasn't experienced the following: a practice member has got behind on the payment of their fees. Months later, they have stopped coming and there is still an outstanding amount.

There are two courses of action:

Chase the money, no matter how much it costs you because you aren't going to let someone get away with cheating you out of your money, time, and professional skills.

OR let the person go with a blessing for their future.

The first is a short-term action to support your business. This costs you in time, focus and often soured relationships. The second is a long-term investment in the person and your business. This often returns way more than the cash value of the money you give away.

There are no rights or wrongs here. Just consider whether you want to go for the possible short-term gain, along with the possible angst, or pay it forward and let the past go with gratitude.

We encourage our coaching clients to choose the latter. If you nurture the person, you create a bond that may (and in our experience does) attract them back when the time is right.

It's a simple act of sending a Write-Off Letter. We use ours at the end of the year. It says something like this:

> *"We've noticed there has been an outstanding amount on your account for quite some time. As we know, this time of year can create financial difficulties for some people, we have decided to clear your balance owing and have closed your case. Your account is now zero. We appreciate having had the opportunity to serve you and wish you all the very best for a prosperous New Year."*

Acts of kindness are often met with warm responses and re-engagements. But it's not just about that. It's about affirming the privilege of serving your practice members and acknowledging the abundance of the world.

Exquisite Delivery doesn't occur when you hold on to the past.

When you let go you grow.

Playtime

- Create your practice's Close Case and Write-Off letters or Download some examples.

Summary

- Choose between chasing the money or letting the person go with a blessing for their future.
- Sending a Write-Off Letter can create a bond and attract people back when the time is right.
- Affirm the privilege of serving your practice members and acknowledge the abundance of the world.
- Letting go helps in growing and achieving exquisite delivery.

Quadrant 4: Energising Expansion

The 8 Strategies of The Attractive Practice Model

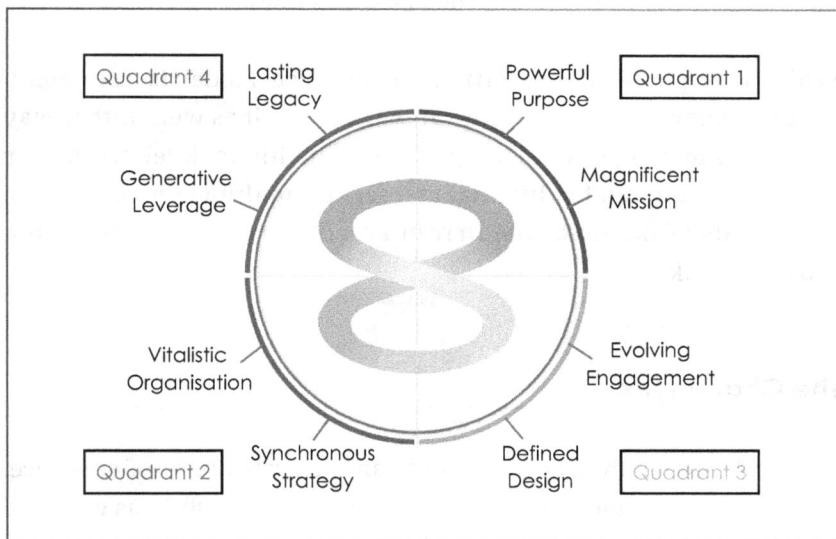

| Quadrant 4 | Lasting Legacy | | Powerful Purpose | Quadrant 1 |

Generative Leverage — Magnificent Mission

Vitalistic Organisation — Evolving Engagement

| Quadrant 2 | Synchronous Strategy | | Defined Design | Quadrant 3 |

The Transition

You have now exited the 'safety zone' of Q's 2 & 3 where life is predictable and safe. You have been shrouded in certainty and protected from harm as you navigated the well-charted waters of practice experience.

You now enter Q4 at your own risk!

The pace will quicken. Risk increases. Options and decisions will be aplenty. You will be awash with paradoxes and counter-intuitive challenges to your very being as the Q4 master of action leads back into the Q1 of possibility as you reinvent your business.

Enter this exciting area of your voyage with a light heart, trusting your vessel and your crew. Make sure you leave your preconceived notions on the shore.

This phase of your practice's voyage will involve you working on the deck less, steering the vessel less and managing the crew less. You will be seeking out high quality talent more, inspiring your team more and reinventing yourself and your business more.

While this phase of the Attractive Practice Model is commonly around expansion and scale, it can be about exit as well. Either way it requires leverage. The leverage covered in this book relates to your team as you build a facility that can service multiple Chiropractors. The details of the Associate Driven Practice System are found in a separate book.

The Challenges

The world is rapidly moving towards an integrated view of existence. We are currently undergoing another transformative shift, as we move to a decentralised and even more interconnected world. It seems like, throughout history, there are decades when not much change occurs, and then decades of change occur in a matter of months. I think we are currently experiencing one of those accelerated cycles of energising expansion.

Our recent progress as inhabitants of this planet began with a Tribal-driven Agrarian Age, a one-dimensional system where the tribal chief or lord of the manor ruled peasants without question.

This gave way to a Hierarchical-driven Industrial Age where those people in ascendancy drove the workers through bureaucracy. This two-dimensional system drove capital and labour to build great things, create strong infrastructure and develop affordable goods and services.

The Knowledge Age that followed has given us the Consensus-driven societies we now experience. Here democracy reigns in the west and information is the primary exchange. This unseen product is controlled by the socially-driven consensus and has taken on a socialistic form. This sets the scene for a more collectivist and communistic method of control for the 'common good' which inevitably will result in an implosion and devolving of the system before the 4th revolution is complete.

In my opinion, the emerging society will be a decentralised, inter-dependent system of intelligence, much of which is virtual, in what may be called the Connection Age. The dawn of personal sovereignty in this decentralised energy network of what could be termed a metaverse will allow for information to be widely spread at the speed of light. This, I believe, is the age that we are entering and as with every paradigm shift, it will not come without resistance from the old order. This technological shift is being accompanied by social, financial and political disruption. This is the course that all revolutions seem to take.

These revolutions occur in cycles. My observation is that a number of cycles of change are converging in this time period, setting us up for a significant shift in our world.

As we enter this new world, we are well advised to draw from the Q4 part of our brain, which carries the wisdom of the preceding three Quadrants. You and your practice will be better off for embracing the paradox produced by the combination of the Tribal, Hierarchical and Consensus paradigms as you journey into a new world of decentralised connection.

All life forms, including your practice, are either growing or dying. Expansion is a process: it is about increments, moment by moment, encounter by encounter, person by person. You don't say, "One day I'll expand." Expansion is a continuous process of leverage, governance and empowerment, and it leaves a legacy.

The opposite to expansion, of course, is contraction. As the saying goes, we are either green and growing or ripe and rotting.

You can't shrink your way to greatness.

The innate desire to grow and expand has been bubbling away within you from the moment you were conceived, but that doesn't mean it comes naturally to the way you practice. The knocks and falls, disappointments and 'failures' of your life journey have created doubt and questions about your ability, and even your entitlement to expansion.

The critical factor here is your choice: do you want to expand? If the answer is yes, then you can learn to bring in your Q4 functions and make it happen.

At all times, are you choosing to expand or to contract? Expansion brings with it a whole new set of challenges, problems and demands for new skills. Many practitioners are afraid of expansion. They're afraid of the personal reinvention required.

So, what is your choice around expansion?

Q4, the driver of expansion, is relatively rare in health practitioners. Only about 5% of the thousands of practitioners who have done the *in8model*® test have had Q4 rise above Q3. Yet, countless numbers of those very same people have found the ability to do it through the Quest Coaching program. They've found what sets their soul on fire and mastered the practice of Q4. Some of them do it by choice.

Sometimes life decides for them; they simply take that moment and meet it with the courage to reinvent and grow.

Emma had a vision for a very caring and gentle chiropractic centre in London, with all women, caring for mothers, babies, and children. Her vision was impeccable. She knew why she was developing this practice. Her systems and processes were strong, and the gaps were identified, and she was working towards fulfilling them. Likewise, her technique was beautiful. She knew what she was doing and delivered it exquisitely, as did her team. They were totally on point.

The challenge for Emma was that a lot of the load was coming back on her shoulders. She needed a finger in every part of the pie, to make sure that everything happened right. As fate would have it, she was about to return from visiting her parents in Australia when the Covid-19 pandemic hit and travel bans sprang up. She was un-able to return to the UK. Thus, she couldn't be in the practice that depended on her. It rested entirely on three associates, who were capable, but who hadn't yet had a chance to step to the next level.

Emma, by necessity, had to grant everyone the power to do what they needed to do to keep the ship afloat. In truth, it was a revolution-ary moment. Other people had to take responsibility for the things she had been doing, and she had to take on the role of governance and business improvement. She has come out of it with a business that didn't suffer under lockdowns. The practice does what it was designed to do, the processes are in place and her associates have ownership. And into the bargain, her Q4 is now firing more than ever. She has the momentum to create another business that will allow her to travel the world and earn an income wherever she may be.

She doesn't have to be putting in massive hours for her practice to thrive. By giving others the ability to thrive, by stepping into the Q4 part, she has given her business wings.

Summary

- The world is rapidly moving towards an integrated view of existence.
- We are undergoing a transformative shift to a decentralised and interconnected world.
- This shift will be met with resistance from the old order and will bring social, financial, and political disruption.
- Individuals and practices should embrace the paradox produced by the Tribal, Hierarchical, and Consensus paradigms in order to navigate this new world.
- It requires personal reinvention and exercise of one's Q4 part.

Quest Procedures For Lifetime Time Care

The 8 Strategies Of The Attractive Practice Model

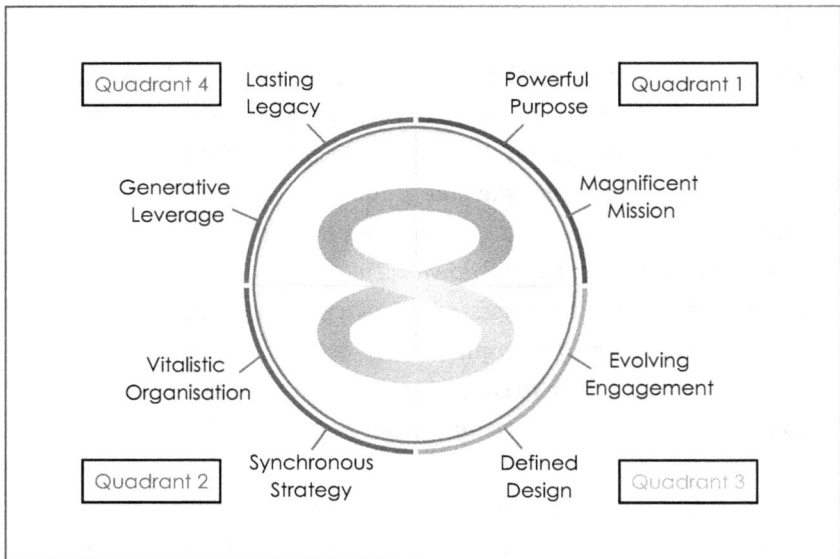

Quadrant 4   Lasting Legacy   Powerful Purpose   Quadrant 1

Generative Leverage   Magnificent Mission

Vitalistic Organisation   Evolving Engagement

Quadrant 2   Synchronous Strategy   Defined Design   Quadrant 3

In the previous three Parts of the QPFLTC, we have been working towards formatting your practice to become the business it can be. Part 4 of the Attractive Practice Model is about Energising Expansion. The procedures we have detailed up until now have given your practice the opportunity to sing from the same song sheet, operate from the same procedures and get some consistency of delivery in a state of excellence.

Now is the opportunity to turn your practice into a business.

This part of the book will give you the chance to leverage other's skills and superpowers so they will duplicate your design. This will benefit your community, your practice members, your team and your business, and free you up to pursue even greater outcomes.

Let's look at the four areas of the QPFLTC as they relate to Energising Expansion.

As noted earlier, each Quadrant of your brain (and your practice) performs a certain function, as identified on the diagram below. Throughout this book we are cycling through Inspiration, Management, Delivery, Reinvention and back to Inspiration, etc., on every aspect of our practice process.

Let's explore this process in the Part 4 context, which is geared towards a Lasting Legacy.

It is the part that brings reinvention to the fore. In this part you get to work on your business, create leverage and expand your reach and contribution.

It empowers all in your circles of influence by challenging people to reach above and beyond what they thought possible.

This part sees the practice becoming less about you and more about the Magnificent Mission you embarked on.

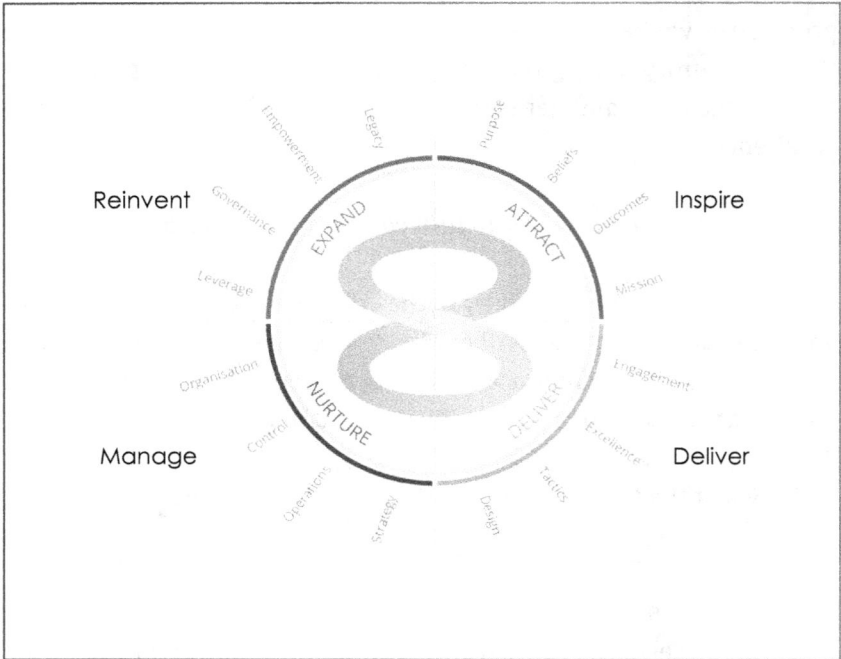

Strategy 7: Generative Leverage

The 8 Strategies Of The Attractive Practice Model

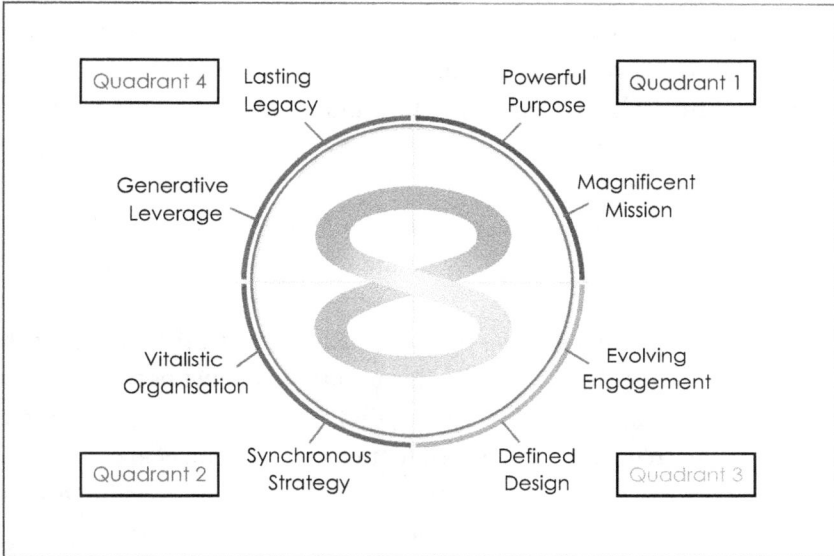

Quadrant 4	Lasting Legacy	Powerful Purpose	Quadrant 1

Generative Leverage

Magnificent Mission

Vitalistic Organisation

Evolving Engagement

Quadrant 2	Synchronous Strategy	Defined Design	Quadrant 3

"Give me a lever long enough and a fulcrum on which to place it, and I shall move the world". Archimedes

Leverage is likely to be the last thing on a chiropractor's mind when they start a shift. However, leverage is the key to expansion. This is easy when one is dealing in a mass-produced product, pushed off the end of a production line. But you are dealing with a relationship-driven, personalised offering. So, how can you leverage that? If you are to scale and expand your practice, you must commit to letting other people and technology help you. The saying, "If you want to go fast, go alone. If you want to go far, go together," encapsulates every expanding practice.

The first profound leverage strategy starts at the point of on-boarding. The first question to ask is, "Who is your who?" When you recognise a character trait, value set or aptitude in a team member and empower it. Then it becomes one of their areas of influence, no matter how new they are to the position.

As I mentioned earlier, technology is a significant part of leverage in our world. However, the pace of technological development is such that if I go into it in this book it will be outdated by the time the book is published. Here we will focus on a slower moving form of leverage – your people. Specifically your team and notably your CA's and paraprofessionals. The topic of associate practice is a whole book on its own. You will find it in the Associate Driven Practice System book.

So, let's dive into the leverage that you will find in your team. As with your practice members it is a matter of building trust between all of your team and having them gain buy-in to all aspects of the practice. Now, this doesn't come for free. All team members must carry responsibility for the area they are empowered in. Otherwise, we have everyone running around feeling good but not necessarily contributing to the practice.

Creating responsibility and accountability for every team member who takes on an area of influence is part of leverage. However, the success or failure of this exercise depends entirely on how willing you are to give over these areas of responsibility.

You can't empower someone and give them responsibility over an area while also micromanaging them.

The focus here is one-to-many. This is your point of leverage. You may be able to do many things really well. Therein lies the block to practice growth. If you insist on doing things that others can do at 80% of your capability you are not allowing your practice to be as Attractive as it could be.

Attraction is compounded from an integrated view of purpose, beliefs, outcomes, and mission, commonly called a culture. When the culture is established you get buy-in from the right people, and they want to come on this journey of discovery with you. You aren't dragging them and you aren't pushing them. You are opening the space for them to join in and further their curiosity, clarity and empowerment, elevating them regardless of whether they are your practice members, CAs or Paraprofessionals.

The culture you create today has a profound affect upon the attractiveness of your practice in the future. When you consider leverage, the big end of town has it sorted. These practices have a steady supply of people wanting to work with them. They do not wake up one day and say, "I need a new team member". They are constantly preparing their practice and more importantly, in this case, they are using their attractive practice as a funnel to take their practice members and move them through a system that produces team members and associates who will work with them in the future.

This section focusses on what is required to set your practice up to ascend yourself and your team, scale your business, and as a result, elevate our profession.

There is always room to reinvent, leverage and expand.

Playtime

- Brainstorm with your team the names of your team and practice members you will assist to ascend, to a level they never dreamed possible.

Summary

- Leverage is key to expansion in chiropractic practice.
- Building trust and buy-in across the team is important for leverage.

- Empower team members based on their character traits, value sets and aptitudes.
- Responsibility and accountability for each team member is crucial for success.
- Micromanaging hinders the leverage process.
- Clarify purpose, beliefs, outcomes, and mission to build attraction.
- Constantly prepare your practice as a funnel to take your team members and move them through a system that produces associates who will come and work with you in the future.
- Invite people to join in a journey of curiosity, clarity, and empowerment.

From One-On-One to Group

If you want to go fast, go alone. If you want to go far, go together.
African Proverb

As practitioners, we employ leverage in many areas. From systems and procedures to administrative assistants to paraprofessional assistants to associates and partners, when we share the load, we get more done with less.

However, at the end of the day, when we are doing the thing we are trained for (caring for people), we are laborers. We earn money from the smarts of our knowledge, the elegance of our touch, the eloquence of our communication and the wisdom of our perspective. It's good money if we do it right, but we have more impact on more people when we turn our hands into a business.

Your tiny practice grew into a little business, which expanded into an energy ready to explode. When your Q4 part comes on the scene, you unleash the business brain and are positioned to use your voice and your mind to create massive leverage and knock it out of the park.

There comes a time when we have accumulated the knowledge, skills and wisdom that allow us to magnify our impact and income by creating content and services that get our message out to a world sorely in need of it.

For me this journey has included having influence in our local community with various clubs and organisations. It continued into professional associations. This is a valuable contribution but is not my preferred method, as gains one can make may be reversed by the next group of board members that succeed you. Contributing to the governance of Chiropractic institutions, on the other hand, has been a productive means of sowing seeds to create change into the future.

Creating Quest as a coaching program for the profession has also proven to be an excellent way to create leverage. Helping others grow themselves and their practices leads to creating world influencers. The track record of Quest Chiropractic Coaching is well established with Chiropractic College Presidents, heads of Chiropractic Associations, College board members and leading researchers among the numbers of people who Quest has been able to assist along their way.

The cool thing is that you don't have to wait until the grey hairs start popping through before you can create the leverage that we speak of. Your practice members are thirsting for your wisdom. Remember that you only have to be one chapter ahead of the audience to be an authority in a given field.

Podcasting, speaking, publishing books and articles are excellent ways that you can guide people's thinking consistent with your narrative.

A super form of leverage in this context is in creating a paid membership group for your practice members. They get a few practice perks, and you share useful content online weekly, organise a get-together once a month or so, and provide a cool resource site. For this, they pay you an appropriate monthly fee.

Playtime

- Identify the area that you will create leverage in.
- Plan your practice members' membership group.

Summary

- Leverage is used in many areas of practice to share the workload.
- As a Chiropractor, you are a labourer earning money from hands-on work.
- Your practice's Q4 section utilises the business brain and creates massive leverage through content and services.
- Influence can be gained through contributing to professional associations and governance of institutions, podcasting, speaking, publishing, and coaching programs.
- Paid membership groups can be created for practice members, providing useful content, practice perks, and other cool stuff, for a monthly fee.

The Paradox of Growth

When I first wrote the original *in8model®* book and the accompanying coaching program, I said to my assistant, "Make sure there is a dot point summary and some suggestions for Playtime at the end of every section." The strong Q4 part doesn't want to do all the reading. In fact, they will probably assign the reading to another person. The Q4 part just wants the bottom line.

The irony behind the Q4 part is that, yes, it does just want the dot point summary and the bottom line, but this is so it can pull things apart and put them together in a new way, and thus drive expansion.

The Q4 part embraces paradox and drives reinvention.

Your practice has the power to change the world. The Q1 part sees and believes in the vision. Your Q2 part manages the systems, data and research that provide the necessary structure. The Q3 part focuses on the art of materialising the vision.

But to take it to the world, we need the Q4 part. Without it, our thinking stays small. We remain dedicated to things that are not effective or efficient uses of our time. If we are to expand in all ways, we must confront the elephants in the room and just GSD.

The Q4 part is both the end of one cycle and the start of a new one. Think of the four parts like the seasons. Winter is Q1, where we engage in internal thought about things to come. Spring is Q2, where new growth comes from seeds planted by Q1. Summer sees the new life forms bearing fruit in the form of Q3. Q4 is the time when the bounty of the cycle is harvested and stored as wisdom and sustenance for the next cycle.

It is here that you will reinvent your practice to be a new version of itself, even if the old version was just fine.

Playtime

- What are the elephants in the room that you are going to deal with to activate more of your Q4 part?
- What are your commitments to reinventing yourself and your practice?

Summary

- Use the dot point summaries in each section of this book.
- The Q4 part seeks the bottom line to drive expansion.
- The Q4 part embraces paradoxes and drives reinvention.

- The Q4 part is needed to confront elephants in the room.
- The Q4 part marks the end of one cycle and start of a new one.
- Immersion in paradoxes and play is required for growth.

Co-opetition

When you read the title of this book, you could be forgiven for thinking that you were about to delve into a meditation-type guide on visualizing yourself into a state of success filled with warm fuzzy vibes. Whilst attraction is indeed a feel-good factor, involving hand holding and cooperation (right brain function), it has as its complementary opposite, the logical, exclusive, and competitive bedrock of business.

The combination of these two opposing parts is where we embrace the paradox of coopetition, or if you would rather, comperation. Yes, your spell checker will go crazy with the joining of these two opposites, but so do the many practitioners who see money as evil or compassion as weak.

Coopetition isn't about being in the middle. It's not a watered-down version of both phenomena. It is a paradigm incorporating the whole practice brain.

The Attractive Practice Model has embraced the paradoxes and exercised the complementary opposites for the benefit of all. It is a practice that engineers competition between team members and at the same time, encourages interdependent cooperation. This combination draws the best from every situation.

Ignorance of the opposites presented by Q1 & 2 and Q3 & 4 can tear people, relationships, organisations, businesses and practices apart, but when they are respected as necessary complementary opposites, expansion flows naturally, and everyone wins.

This is the essence of coopetition.

Playtime

• Where do you see the similarities and opposites in others as non-useful and what are you going to do about it?

Summary

• Attraction is important but it needs the complementary opposites of both logic and competition.
• The combination of these two opposing parts is where we play in the world of comperation or coopetition.
• Comperation/coopetition is not a watered-down version of both, but a paradigm that incorporates the whole practice brain.
• The Attractive Practice Model embraces the paradoxes and exercises the complementary opposites for the benefit of all.
• Ignoring the complementary opposites can cause damage to people, relationships, organizations, businesses and practices.

Be The Chairperson

You can't grow your practice by just doing more of what got you to where you are. You do it by engaging your Q4. You do it by being the chairman of the board: the inspirator and big picture thinker, a leader able to engage the left-brained part. You ask questions: how do we do this better, more effectively, more efficiently, in a new way, to save time, to save resources, to increase the bottom line, etc.?

A word of warning. When you engage your Q4 part, you are dealing with a very powerful energy, which can be scary to other parts, especially the Q3 part, both yours and other people's. It is important to be aware of others' differences and play with them accordingly.

Susan, a coaching client of ours, did a great job of negotiating this challenge.

Susan is a 'Get Stuff Done' sort of lady, full of big vision and a can do attitude. Intent on her outcomes, she often appeared abrupt and blunt when dealing with people. With that comes a certain necessary obnoxiousness. Her high staff turnover did leave clues but she tended to blame it on people's incompetence and lack of drive.

Through some very direct coaching (which she appreciated), she realised her direct approach with her team and practice members was holding her back from taking her practice to the next level.

She realised that there was power in the soft, touchy-feely that was so not her. To her credit, she work diligently (with the help of her team) on softening her approach, praising and acknowledging others.

To her surprise the energy of the practice lifted, team attrition decreased and the bottom line jumped up.

Always remember, you do have all parts within and we don't do all parts equally. Sometimes, however it is useful to use a 'not me' part in order to empower and bring out the best in others.

Playtime

- What are you afraid of in your Q4 part?
- Which is your most unused part and how could it be useful for you to apply it.

Summary

- The Q4 part of the business requires you to switch from the practitioner to the chairperson role.
- Let go and empower others with purpose, plans, procedures, and expansion resources.

- Growing the practice involves engaging Q4 and being a big-picture thinker and leader.
- Be aware of others' differences, especially the Q3 part.
- Just because we have all parts within doesn't mean we have to do all parts equally.

Governance – the View from Thirty Thousand Feet

Some things in business and practice are not terribly obvious if they are present and functioning. However, they are bleedingly obvious if they are absent. Policies, procedures, reports, responsibilities, team cohesion and buy in to the big mission are all such things.

Expansive governance is like this, too. But here's the catch: many of the governance functions sit comfortably within the purview of Q2. However, when we look at these tools from a place of Q4 governance, rather than a place of management, we see things significantly differently.

The catch is that you need both but in what proportions?

When you are managing a practice, you need to monitor and review all areas of performance regularly. That's a given. You need to have measurement tools in place so you can create clarity, control and accountability. These tools feed into your key performance indicators, your critical numbers, and your organisational scorecards.

I have sat on a number of company boards and noticed big differences in style. One tertiary board I contributed to use the analogy that management is like looking at the carpet on the floor and planning activities around the dead bugs stains, whilst governance is like looking out the window, visioning and planning the future. As a board, we would remind ourselves and each other whenever we were spending too much time in our deliberations in either place. It always got us back on track.

Governance takes the conversation up a level. Here, we are moving from the hindbrain survival control mechanism, to the forebrain, and its infinite opportunities and possibilities. In doing so, we take the reports, numbers and scorecards and ask what they are telling us about the subject of discussion.

We ask what they are telling us about our people and practice members. We ask whether every action is coherent with our mission and purpose. We ask where we are being let down, what we need to shed, and what we need to implement.

Management handles the necessary detail of the day-to-day, while governance takes a helicopter view and asks where all this information sits in the bigger picture. This overview is essential to perspective and appropriate proactive directorship.

The Governance Map

The impetus and energy behind the Expand function lead and inspire in a way that creates forward momentum. The governance aspect of this makes it measurable, analysable, and concrete. The information flows down through the system, going from the big picture, the concepts and values, down through the principles that you live and operate by, to the details of the day-to-day operations. This cascade provides an opportunity for the essence of the practice to be infused into every function at the coalface.

The energy of governance frees up the visionaries to imagine, the managers to manage and the workers to work. It's always about keeping the ship sailing smoothly towards its destination, with the big mission and the big problem we are here to solve in mind.

The Q4 and Q1 parts set the big picture objectives, which are taken by the Q2 part and translated into eight-week targets and fourteen-day goals that the rest of the business can work with.

The following is a series of functions in this cascade that we use with our coaching clients. This provides a holistic process for governing your business. Some of these points have been covered in the earlier chapters and some are listed for you to explore yourself. If you have any questions don't hesitate to reach out to us at Quest.

- **Core Values** (The core values are your team's top 10 or so values. These are expressed in an operational form usually in a short sentence often punctuated with a relevant adjectives)
- **Urgent Problem** (The thing in the world that you are repulsed by)
- **Unique Solution** (Your local solution to the Urgent Problem)
- **Affirmational Statement of Purpose** (Your super big statement of what your practice is, who your team are, who you serve (taken from the Ideal Practice Member))
- **Mission Statement** (Watered down or politically correct version of your Affirmational Statement of Purpose)
- **Practice Member's Point of Pain** (What drives your practice members to continuously engage with you?)
- **Ideal Practice Member** (Your Avatar and how you work with them to help them realise their potential)
- **Team Members' Point of Pain** (What your team member/s yearn for)
- **Ideal Team** (Your ideal team members and how you will progress them to ascend)
- **Manifesto** (Your gutsy, polarising and loud statement of your stand)
- **Elevator Pitch** (Your short statement about what you do)
- **Positioning Statement** (Your short tagline associating your practice with a lofty concept)
- **Promise to our people** (Your eye-to-eye promise that you make to your practice member)

- **Critical Number** (Your one or two key metrics that indicate how the practice is going)
- **4 Quadrant Functions** (The current self-ratings of the Quadrants of your business brain)

The 4 Quadrant Functions

When it comes to the day-to-day function of your practice make sure that you only take on those tasks you are able to address in a given time frame. Most chiropractors underestimate the time it takes to accomplish a task, resulting in distress when timeframes or budgets blow out. We suggest an 8-week cycle of activity based on the current priorities within the 4 Quadrant Functions.

Give your practice a score from 0-5 in each Quadrant, and commit to the activities that will move the needle the most.

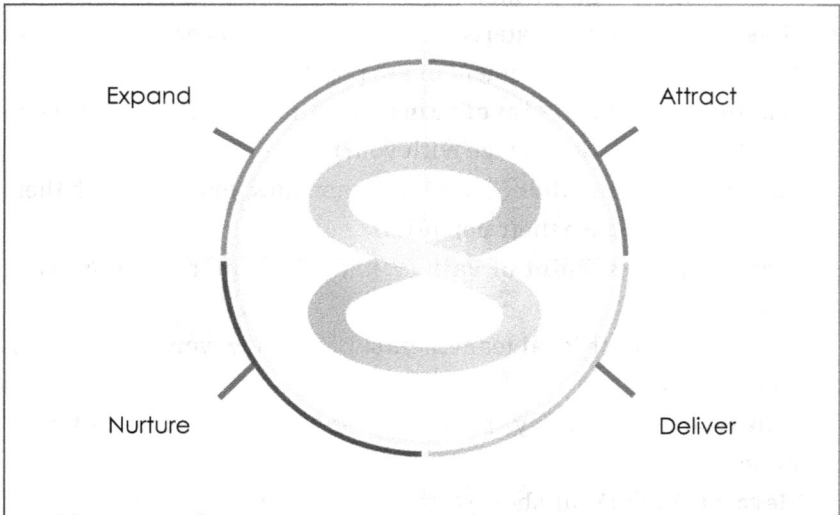

- **One Year Objectives**
  - **Financial** (Your gross revenue last year and this year)
  - **Critical Number** (Your key measurable statistic, which will probably be total services last year and this year).
- **8 Week Targets**
  - Identify what you could possibly do in the next 8 weeks to move towards your one year objectives.
  - Now look at what you realistically WILL do in the next 8 weeks to attain this target. (Assign an accountable person to each target.)
- **14 Day Goals**
  - Identify what you could possibly do in the next 14 days to move towards your 8 Week target.
  - Now look at what you realistically WILL do in the next 14 days to attain this target.
- **Weekly Check-ins**
  - Have brief interactions on a weekly basis to ensure that the 14 day goals are on track.
- **Daily Huddles**
  - Have a huddle before and after every shift to ensure that time and opportunities are optimised.

Playtime

- Are your next 8 weeks' activities realistic and attainable?

Finances

Many dedicated Chiropractors love their art so much that they'd do it for free if they could! And yet, at some point, they have to face up to the reality that money matters.

Money represents energy. The practitioner puts energy into studying and honing their skills, and time into delivering the services, for
which the recipient gives the equivalent value in the form of money.

The energy of money allows you to do more in the world, but money is
not wealth. It's what it buys that is wealth.

Many people think fee systems are about covering costs and making
a profit, but there is far more to it than that. The old proverb says,
"Where your treasure is, there your heart is." When you enter into a
relationship with your practice members, you are exchanging value.
Thus, you need to consider more than market value, costs, and profit
margins when you set your fees.

There are four elements that we introduced at the beginning of the
book that drive your practice and definitely affect your fee system.

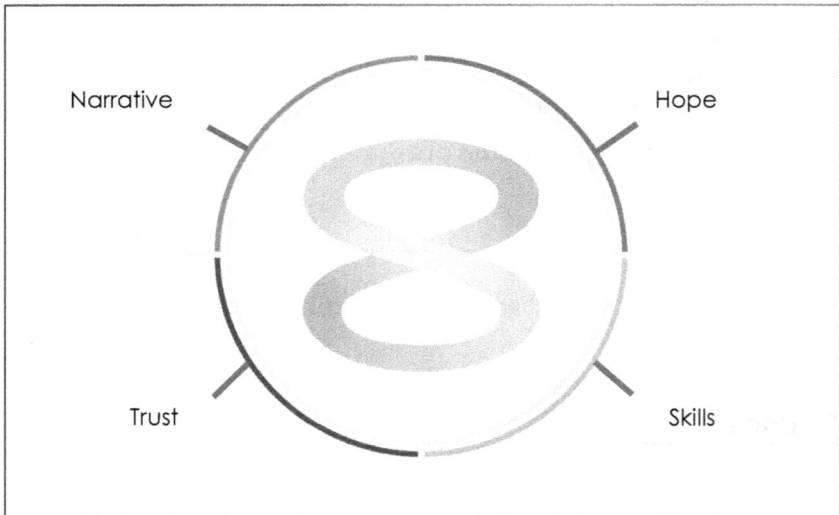

Narrative

Hope

Trust

Skills

Q1 – Hope

The energy of hope for a better future gives a person something to live for. A better tomorrow. A better outcome. Always make sure your interactions with every person you encounter are filled with hope and possibility. This is not just a placebo; it has a significant impact on a person's neurology.

Q2 – Trust

Trust is continually being earned and spent. The degree of nurture increases the value. This is represented by your practice's organisation, consistency and authenticity. It is often not what you say but the questions you ask that stimulate others to critically assess their own awareness, enhancing their trust in you and your practice.

Q3 – Skills

Your ability to create your offering in a way that is useful to others. This includes your rapport, bedside manner and associated tone of communication as well as your technical skills.

Q4 – Narrative

The ability to challenge people to bigger ways of thinking or action gives massive returns. People come to you for more than a transaction. When they realise that your practice calls them to a higher version of themselves, they will do whatever it takes and pay whatever it costs to get what you have got.

Your fee system must consider all of these elements, and be tailored to the specific practice members you love to serve. The fee system, then, is reflective of your philosophy. Who do you want to serve and what do they find the attractive parts of your offering? Do they want inspiration for the future, a knowledgeable authority, a deep connection with their care giver or bottom-line results in a timely manner?

People also shift in their wants and needs as their journey with you evolves, so you must be ready to shift your value exchange methods as appropriate.

When someone first walks through the door of your practice, they may be desiring relief from a symptom of some sort. They will probably be focussed on results. They will pay full fee at this time. There are two fee options here:

1. Pay visit by visit

The negative here is that people paying at the point of sale costs time and labour and a loss of CA efficiency.

The positive is that the time spent results in improved relationships with your CAs. If people stop at the front desk every visit, they develop relationships with your CAs. They get to know, like and trust your team. This goes a long way towards them making bigger and longer commitments for their care.

2. Pre or Post Pay

The negative here is that people often confuse the financial incentives associated with longer term payment systems with the clinical recommendations for their care. So, when the payments for a block of care conclude, people assume that their clinical activities are at an end, and they leave.

The positive is that it is easy and time saving (with the right systems) to process a person on any given visit, preventing log jams at the front desk and making the most of CAs' time.

We recommend that you consider the first phase of care as the opportunity to really get to know the new person. Using the pay as you go system provides the new practice member with the maximum possible contact.

Once they get into higher levels of care, they qualify for financial plans that allow them easy access in and out of the practice, as all the details are handled automatically.

As the months and years go by, and life becomes even brighter, they know that the connection they have with you and the skill you bring to every situation are integral parts of a healthy lifestyle. They then become eligible for your top tier club, or as we refer to it, the Healthy Lifestyles Club.

This is not providing a discount as an incentive for people to use care. It is a recognition of people who value their care. At this level, you may also give them other items of value – information, mentoring, discounts on products, or even just connection with other practice members in the Club.

Think of the ways that you can add to the offerings of this loyalty club? This level may provide a reduced fee on the Post Pay system, or maybe a fixed fee for unlimited services. People are offered this based on the status of their clinical achievements, and all people are given the same fee (babies through to the elderly).

To calculate your fees, decide what average fee you want and increase it or decrease it, giving a fee reduction to those in the higher level of care (Optimisation Care), and increasing fees for people in the lower level (Stabilisation Care), therefore attaining your desired average fee.

It is always a challenge to find the right average fee. We suggest that you test your market by increasing your fee in increments until you find the resistance point. This is a test and measure phenomena which must be rolled out over a time span of many months. Fees will vary greatly between countries, states, regions and even suburbs but don't get sucked in to just going along with what everyone else is charging – your practice and it's offering is unique.

This fee system is part of management by *agreement*, ensuring valuable exchange is offered at every level. But it is also part of building a tribe of people who resonate with your practice culture. Remember, you are not about selling a product or service.

Playtime

- Ensure that your fee system reflects fair exchange for the services that you offer.
- Test your market for fee resistance.
- Decide on the models of fees for the various stages of care.

Summary

- Money represents energy in the exchange of services between practitioners and clients.
- Money is not wealth. Rather, what it buys is wealth.
- Fee systems should consider more than market value, costs and profit margins when determining pricing.
- Four elements that drive a practice and affect fee systems are hope, trust, skills, and narrative.
- The fee system should be tailored to your clients' and your community's evolving wants and needs.

Contribution

Contribution could be said to be the reason that you do what you do. We are all here to make a unique and lasting contribution to the world. You have assets and as a chiropractor, they are profound and long-lasting.

Your contribution in many areas may not be evident to you in your lifetime, but know that you cannot NOT make a contribution – you can only assume that you are contributing, and the effects will be evident in the fullness of time.

Let's look at the elements of contribution via the in8model®

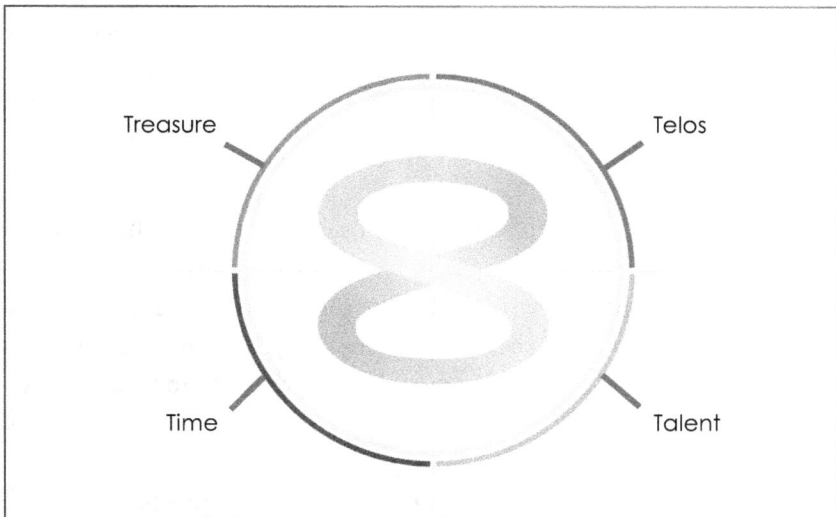

Q1 – Telos

The word "telos" is a Greek term that can be translated to mean "end", "purpose" or "goal". It is often used in philosophy, particularly in Aristotle's works, to refer to the ultimate end or purpose of something, even of human existence. For example, the telos of a human being might be seen as the achievement of happiness or virtue.

Get clear on your telos.

Q2 – Time

Time is one of our most precious resources. It is limited; once it's gone, it cannot be regained. Time can be managed and allocated to different projects or tasks to increase productivity and contribution. Your management of time, and specifically your management of your energy within your time, ensures that your telos is expressed appropriately.

Infuse your telos into your time so you are present every moment.

Q3 – Talent

You have unlimited talent at your disposal. As well as your personal super powers, you have your people, friends, peers, team, practice members and community. Tap into your field of talent and you'll find a treasure trove of resources to help amplify your contribution. This is what you create if you decide to scale your practice to be an Associate Driven Practice.

Invest your telos and your time into your collective talent.

Q4 – Treasure

Over your time as a chiropractor you will accumulate much wealth and treasure, as long as you practice these four elements of contribution. Make sure that you don't spend more than you earn and always play the long game. Resist the temptation to go for quick wins and short term gains. Seed your treasure into those people, businesses, organisations, associations and institutions that represent your values. Wealth requires repetition over time, so be strategic and persistent with your projects of saving, investing and tithing.

Put your telos, time, talents and treasures to work so that your impact, influence and contribution will be felt far and wide.

Playtime

- Define your telos in your Statement of Purpose.
- Arrange your time allocations in your Default Diary.
- Identify and strategise your talent resources.
- Design and implement your treasure accumulation and seeding plans.

Summary

- We are all here to make a unique and lasting contribution to the world.
- Telos, the Greek term for "end", "purpose" or "goal", is important for understanding one's contribution.
- Time is a precious resource that can be managed and allocated to increase productivity and contribution.
- Talent is unlimited, and it can be used to amplify one's contribution.
- Support the people, businesses, organizations, and institutions that align with your values.
- To maximise one's impact, influence and contribution, it is important to infuse telos into time, talent, and treasure.

Empowerment

Every person is at their own level of competence. They are available to ascend to their next level. Some choose to and others don't – yourself included.

The people and actions that got you to where you are now will *not* get you to where you want to be next, so you owe it to your business to constantly challenge and empower yourself and your team (including your practice members) to excel at their next level.

To generate a sustainable practice which runs on its own momentum, your attractive practice must become an institution that is constantly ascending to higher levels of impact and contribution. This business can then create prosperity without your direct involvement.

When we move into the Q4 Expand function, we are thinking about people. We are thinking about how we build people and journey with them in a practical way.

It is a question of empowerment. Does your practice empower every person it encounters? Do your report forms create conversations that elevate people, whether they be practice members and their friends and family or your team members? Does your practice environment create talking points, through posters, videos, questionnaires, assessments or the like? Is every team member growing on an individual level as they journey through their time in your practice?

Remember that they will leave you when they outgrow you or when their values are no longer in alignment with yours. You can only lead people as far as you are willing to go. How are you empowering yourself?

You and each of your team members have huge talent dwelling within. Talent, when released, will take your practice to the next level. The challenge lies in the HOW of empowering people. You are in the business of growing your people. This is a long-term proposition, so be kind to yourself and others when it comes to how high you set the bar.

Let's look at four key elements to empowerment of people in your practice.

1. Your Expectations

Your rules (read expectations) for others will influence the way you interact with them. Often we expect of others that which we expect of ourself. This makes for unrealistic and maybe unattainable outcomes for others, and frustration for us. Know where a team member is and where you would like to take them, and be clear on both your and their expectations.

2. Hire right

Know that Character always comes before skills. Making a poor hiring choice is the cost that keeps on costing. Have the team do the in-8model® quiz so you are aware of their preferred behaviours and their empowerment processes.

3. Optimise people's strengths and place people appropriately

Teaching fish to run and eagles to dance is frustrating and non-productive for all. Certain people are at their best in certain roles, so have them playing in their sweet spot wherever possible. The *in8model®* quiz results indicate where these spots may lie.

4. Create an environment that brings out the best in people

Create an elastic environment. A little bit of competition and a little bit of cooperation give people a chance to stretch and strengthen and become more competent but not too cockie. Remember that environment affects behaviour, so create a meaningful environment for your team and your practice members.

Giving and receiving feedback of the right type, in the right amounts, at the right time, lets people grow together. Make sure that the feedback is sandwiched between praise and pre-framing. Ensure that every person you deal with is always becoming more empowered.

Attractive practices are made up of attractive people who in turn attract other attractive people to join them. You don't get your team to perform through motivation. You set up an inspirational environment and watch them pop to new levels of personal greatness.

Playtime

- Have a plan for the empowerment of every team member.
- Have an ascension plan for many of your practice members, especially those who will become chiropractors.

Summary

- Every person is doing a level of competence and can choose to ascend to their next level.
- To excel in business, it is important to constantly challenge and empower oneself and one's team.
- A sustainable practice should be an institution that constantly ascends to higher levels of impact and contribution.
- Empowerment is key to building people and journeying with them in a practical way.
- Know where each team member is and where you would like to take them, and be clear on both your and their expectations.
- Have the team do the in8model® quiz so you are aware of their preferred behaviours and their empowerment processes.
- Optimise people's strengths and place them appropriately.
- You don't get your team to perform through motivation.
- You set up an inspirational environment and watch them pop to new levels of personal greatness.

Strategy 8: Lasting Legacy

The 8 Strategies Of The Attractive Practice Model

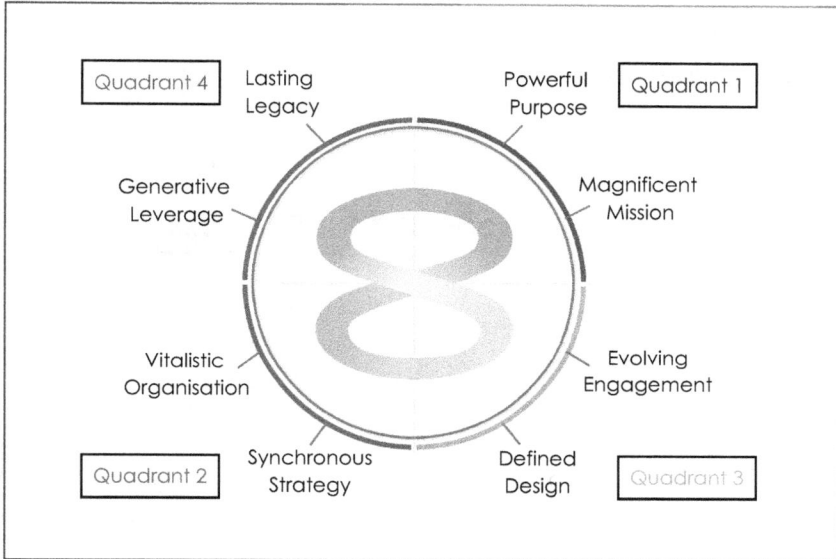

Quadrant 4 | Lasting Legacy | Powerful Purpose | Quadrant 1

Generative Leverage

Magnificent Mission

Vitalistic Organisation

Evolving Engagement

Quadrant 2 | Synchronous Strategy | Defined Design | Quadrant 3

This section addresses getting momentum, going far and going together. Creating an environment where purpose permeates your whole business results in a lasting legacy. The team has an innate ownership of the culture, and people do the right thing without having to be highly managed. Accountability is across the board, and everyone honours their roles and responsibilities.

The cross-pollination of the model enables the business to continue way beyond the departure of any one person, including its original owner. This enables the dream you have for your enterprise to flourish into the future with or without you.

The lasting legacy is in the people we influence along the way. I have had the privilege of conceiving and developing a number of practices in my professional journey. It is so rewarding to see what they have developed into as they gather their own steam.

You have the opportunity to affect so many people by what you say and do, and I may add, don't say and don't do.

Remember, you are playing the long game to create something that lives on long after you do.

The 4 Seasons of Your Business

The 4 Seasons of Your Business

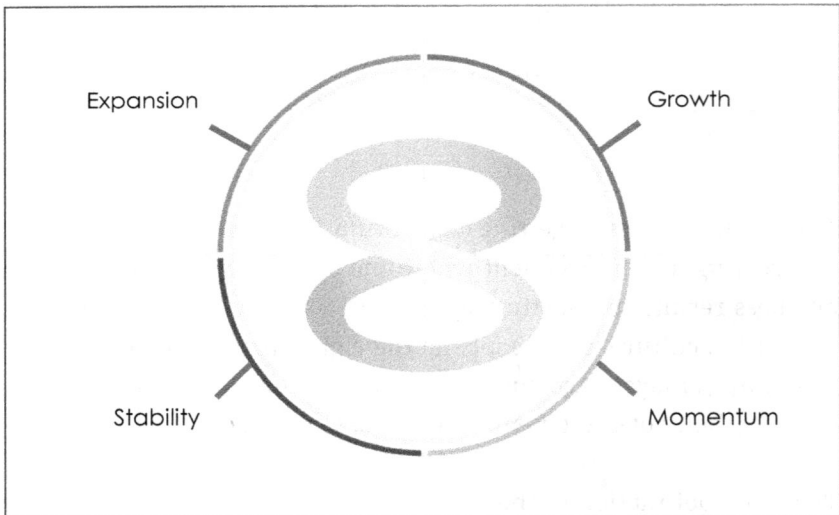

Season 1 – Growth

When you graduate, the chances are that you are well-intentioned, with a life-changing skillset at your disposal. You just want to learn as much of the practical, hands-on stuff as possible. You love the why, what, and how of what you do as a practitioner. You are a content professional, doing what you are trained for. Business is good – people flood in to see you. You attend to them and most of them get great results. As long as *you* pump it everything works – yes, as long as *you* are on the job, *you* keep the plates spinning and all is good. *You* are in control.

Season 2 – Stability

There comes a time, though when you run into limits to the practice's growth as a business. You realise you have to work out better systems to ensure that bills get paid on time, overheads are met, and systems are refined to make everyone's experience seamless. There is a time when the practice needs something that is not the superpower of most practitioners. Playing in the world of having to organise fine detail, pay wages, write policy, and micromanage staff is not your dream – this is *not* what you went to university to do. As discussed earlier, being the CEO is not the natural fit for most practitioners.

Just because you can *do it all, doesn't mean you* should.

Season 3 – Momentum

The next question is WHO can do these things that you can do but don't love? You surrender to the vulnerability of trusting others to do the work in some of your unloved areas. You ensure that every person on your team is empowered to carry out their role. You resist the urge to micromanage and you find that by reducing the hierarchy and leveling the business to a lateral playing field, you empower others to take control of their areas of passion. This allows your practice to gain momentum, and frees you up to direct the business.

Season 4 – Expansion

You ascend to the role of chair of the board and surround yourself with others much smarter than you. You cast the vision, set the compass for the practice's true north and sail the ship towards the chosen destination. You don't have to be the king or queen of the day-to-day minutiae. Here lies the secret to attraction-based growth and the practice of your dreams.

Playtime

- What is your design for your practice's long game?
- What season is your practice in right now?

Summary

- Creating a lasting legacy means creating an environment where purpose permeates the whole business, and everyone has ownership of the culture and does the right thing.
- The cross-pollination of the business model enables it to continue beyond the departure of any one person.
- In season 1 the practitioner is well-intentioned, loves what they do, and the business is good.
- In season 2 the practitioner runs into the limits of the practice's growth as a business and needs to work out better systems.
- In season 3 the practitioner trusts others to take control of their areas of responsibility.
- In season 4 the practitioner becomes the chairman of the board, casting the vision and sailing the ship towards the chosen destination.

Constant Improvement

A business is always broken. It's a constant process of spinning plates. As in life, we are either growing or we are dying – we cannot occupy a state in between. The Attractive Practice Model is constantly in a state of becoming. Your practice is a dynamic, vitalistic living organism – it's not just a bunch of mechanical parts.

So, let's have a look at some of the essential ingredients of growing your team.

Focus

The first challenge for many chiropractors is to focus on the one thing that will move the practice forward the most. When new coaching clients join us, they are like kids in a candy store when they get access to the Quester Center resources. They want to sample every corner of our extensive library of content. Consuming hundreds of videos and downloads will surely lead to overwhelm or exhaustion, and certainly won't get done the one or two things that would make the biggest difference. Invariably, the new client will come around to setting up a rhythm of tasks, only taking on what they can realistically get done in an 8 week cycle. These are set at the Intensives, held every two months.

For improvement to be sustainable and constant, the distractions of the day-to-day pressure and noise (both external and internal) be minimised. In the controlled Q2 space, you will be able to focus on the information and strategy needed to move towards your identified tasks.

The final step is to set an allocated timeframe to achieve completion of the component tasks that will move your practice forward. A default diary is a big help to allocate dedicated times for getting certain things completed.

A Systematised Process of Delivery

When a person has a clear pathway for doing certain things, they feel comfortable and capable of following the appropriate steps. We owe it to our team to have every step of the practice members' journey prescribed. This allows everyone concerned to know exactly what has happened, what is going on now and what is required next.

The Quest Procedures for Lifetime Care, as outlined in this book, are a tried and tested system that ushers your practice members, your team and your associates through their ascendance of care levels and educational distinctions within your practice. Also bear in mind that what worked yesterday or last year may not work today or in the future. A practice requires constant tweaking and redesigning. Herein lies some challenges with the associates with Q2 or 3 preferences, who may be resistant to change. Ensure that changes in your systems are thoroughly explained and linked to your practice's values, so that you get team buy in.

The Voyage

In all growth processes there are foundational functions that must be sorted for higher level functions to be effective. Business building is no exception. The foundational aspects of the QPFLTC must be in place for the ascension components to work consistently. The chart of the Voyage is a time-tested ascension pathway for chiropractic practices.

The Voyage

THE VOYAGE CHART

Quest
CHIROPRACTIC COACHING

PV /Month	Income /Month	Income /Year	ATTRACT	NURTURE	DELIVER	EXPAND
1500	87,000	$1 mil+	• Curiosity • The Next Iteration • Collaborative Partnerships	• Operations Manager • Publish • Scientific Contribution	• Optimisation of Resources • Clinical Contribution to Profession • Wayshower Governance	• Political Influence • Growing Legacy • Equity Sell-Offs
1300	75,400	$900k	• Completion • Generative Sessions • Patterns	• Impact on Profession • Playing the Long Game • Board of Directors	• Branded by Technique • Chiropractic Finishing School • Internal Mentoring	• Multiple Income Streams • Compensation • Business Model 301
1100	63,800	$760k	• Community • Congruence • Events Driven Practice	• Profitability • Team Empowerment • in8model - Associates	• Team Ascension • Executive Assistant • Personal Care - 301	• Communication - 301 • Financial Contribution • Recurring Income
900	52,200	$625k	• Redesign • PM Ascension • Attracting Associates	• Practice Layout • Associate Driven Practice • OPM - Expand	• Transferable Protocols • Contact Hours/% of Income • Personal Care - 201	• Free Up A DAy • Investment Strategies • Seeding Practices
700	40,600	$490k	• Communication 201 • Cultivating Chiropractors • Team Centered Mission	• Debt Reduction • Operational Cascade • OPM -Deliver	• Time & Motion • Meetings that Matter • Tech CA	• Statistics • Wealth Building • Business Model 201
500	29,000	$350k	• Physical Marketing • Culture • Client Centered Mission	• 3rd Phase - Optimisation Care • in8model - Business • OPM - Nurture	• Educational Plan • Internal Referrals • Personal Care 101	• Default Diary • Holidays • Congruence
300	17,400	$210k	• Annual Marketing Plan • The Journey - QPFLTC • Automated Lead Generation	• 2nd Phase - Regenerative Care • Storyboards • OPM - Attract	• Clinical Clarity • State Control • Communication - 101	• The Super CA • Management • Business Model 101
200	11,600	$140k	• Purpose, Outcomes • Bay 5 - Mission • Bay 1 - Beliefs	• 1st Phase - Stabilisation Care • Bay 6 - Strategy • Bay 2 - Organisation	• Visits 1&2 • Bay 7 - Design • Bay 3 - Engagement	• Money • Bay 8 - Leverage • Bay 4 - Empowerment

* Based on per visit of 58

© MJ, 2022 v2.1

257

Ensure that you can honestly check off the foundational functions that sit below your service/income band before moving up to the next level.

A Plan for Team Improvement

We are all on a journey of discovery. We are becoming more of who we are and realising our potential as people.

Part of your role as an owner of your business is to orchestrate the personalised journey for your team. It should be fashioned for the needs of the individual team member. Know where you want to take them and reveal the components of the journey along the way.

Leave A Lasting Legacy

Just the other day, Peter, a chiropractor we coach, excitedly told me that one of his young practice members had announced that he'd realised that his name is all over chiropractic. He loves it, it's shifted his life's direction, and he's now in the process of enrolling at chiropractic college. The cool thing about this was that this young man had only started in the practice a few months before. He had come in looking for a quick fix for a sore knee. He'd wanted only one visit, but by the time he'd experienced the philosophy, science and artistry that Peter conveyed, his life had pivoted in totally unexpected ways.

It gives me a thrill to hear such things, because, beyond all the physical and reputational aspects of legacy, it is the people who will carry it forward. They will make sure that what you do gets passed on and becomes a lasting legacy. Who knows. This youngster could be a future leader of the profession, or something even greater.

Recently, David, the chiropractor with whom I began my practice journey as a new graduate, passed away. I had the honour of delivering an acknowledgement of his well-lived life during a seminar attended by hundreds of chiropractors.

Troy, an acknowledged master in his particular field of chiropractic, was one of the presenters. I recalled the day when Troy first presented at our practice as a newborn, back in the 1970s, and David first adjusted him.

I showed the audience a recent photo of Troy and David, taken when the 92-year-old David had just been adjusted by Troy at his regular visit, a short time before he died.

David left a legacy which goes way beyond him. I felt humbled by the heartfelt appreciation expressed by the large audience, many of whom had been directly influenced by David's life. This is a profound example of the chiropractic circle of life.

The age-old challenge in life and business is to stay relevant at all times. As we know, everything is changing, always. Everything is temporary. To remain relevant, it is critical that you notice the changes and adjust, as people, practices, businesses and in fact, the world shift.

Know that every business is built to sell, so get used to tracking your net asset value and making decisions around how much you invest in and take from your business. When is the time to sell down on the value and what means will you use to do so?

The complexities of a practice's sale is vast and we cover this in the Associate Driven Practice book. If you have specific needs in this area contact us and we can help get these formulas and mechanisms right.

- If you are interested in the Associate Driven Practice System, you will find it in the Resources. It will save you time, money, and much trial and error.

Looking Toward the Future

The disagreements over competing details of techniques, viewpoints and methods have been reputed to be a stumbling block for our profession. They may feel uncomfortable, and it could be argued that they hold us back, but maybe they are really important.

The sanitization of humanity has been going on for a generation or two. Things have to be politically correct. If you happen to have a different viewpoint from the main narrative, you are labelled as unclean.

You will be attacked if you don't fit into the current politically correct narrative. That doesn't apply to just chiropractic. There are hordes of differing viewpoints at the highest levels of science that are scorned just like chiropractic has been for nigh on 130 years. This is just part of the game.

Chiropractic, as a cause, is larger than all of us. It is larger than the philosophy, science, art and politics that we are taught. As we ascend, we become more aware that we are a part of an immense field of energy, a universal intelligence that envelops us. The whole earth vibrates in it and through our intuition, we broadcast and receive from it.

Chiropractic is not just a therapy or a modality. It's a construct that helps people realise their magnificence. It is one with the human potential movement. If you are able to see the person as whole, integrated, a picture of spiritual, mental, physical, and emotional wellbeing, that is manifested not only in their symptomatology but also in their full expression of energy, aspirations and accomplishments, you can see how chiropractic contributes to the journey of life.

Taking someone from a disempowered, dislocated, devolved human being to one who, after a few chiropractic adjustments rejoices in the privilege of being alive, is nothing short of amazing. When people see the gift in their symptoms and enthusiastically enrol in the journey of expressing their life force, they see the world as a place of safety, joy and love.

You Are At A Defining Moment In History.

I believe that our profession sits at crossroads. We can define ourselves by the lowest common denominator, what we DO. Sure, we do many things with our myriad of techniques and we do see amazing results (with back pain, neck pain, headaches, indigestion, ADHD, cancer, you name it). But this is not who we ARE – it's not who you are.

You are an empowered, unique individual, seeing the perfection of the world, bringing your own unique offering to the table. When you work on this wavelength, chiropractic is a metaphor for life – it's the way you express your purpose, and it makes you sing. This energy attracts people to you like bees around a honey pot.

The defining moment, therefore, is every moment. It's the way you get out of bed in the morning, and every interaction during your day – every person you encounter, every adjustment, every word you utter, every decision you make and every action you take. The ripple effect of your actions every moment defines the present and the future.

Are you just another healthcare worker, competing for the attention of patients? No! You are unique, and you live in a world that needs you. Your zest for life vibrates at a distinct frequency and attracts like-minded people to your tribe.

If you look at the Einsteins, Teslas and Edisons of history, they were driven by huge passions for possibilities and potentials. In their cases, these potentials lay within the deductive areas of science. They may have started their explorations looking at the minutia, but they transcended that and saw the bigness within all. They left a massive contribution to the world because they worked *differently*.

Current science has become extremely inductive, with massive commercial and political constraints. Chiropractic, on the other hand, has the beautiful philosophical position that we are more than our bodies. We are a spark of Innate Intelligence, within the field of Universal Intelligence. The discovery of DD Palmer in 1895, expressed in his 1910 book, 'The Science, Art and Philosophy of Chiropractic', was that Chiropractic is "Founded On Tone."

It's Tone. It's Energy. It's Vibration. It's the Whizz, It's the Spizz.
It's the Attractiveness of Chiropractic and of YOU, the Chiropractor.

That's what chiropractic is about. It's founded on tone and defined through the 33 Principles of Chiropractic, laid down by Ralph W. Stephenson D.C. in 1927 in his book, 'The Chiropractic Textbook'. Sure, they are written in the language of the day, and some parts have been updated as science has advanced, but the core premise remains that matter is an expression of energy. Tone is central to our work as chiropractors. We are here to raise the tone, so the physical can reunite with the spiritual, and the finite is dissolved into the infinite.

The masses sit in a putrefying bog of low vibration, while the thinkers, the thought leaders, and the movers and shakers look at things differently and stretch the boundaries. They are few in number but massive in effect.

Chiropractic is meant for this high vibrational space.
Are you?

Ascension Coaching with Quest

Perhaps it needs to be acknowledged here that if Q4 doesn't come naturally to you, a coach can be the pattern interrupt that takes you from "one day I'll expand" to a place of readiness and action.

The pull of old patterns of beliefs and insecurities rather than leaning forward into optimistic reinvention is something that a good coach can break you out of. They become a vessel for the creation and channelling of ideas, and they create accountability for you to move forward.

The in8model® coaching within Quest Chiropractic Coaching will bring the considerations in from the Q2 part that says "Okay, but what do you need to shed in order to grow in this new area?" They then channel the Q3 part that says "What do I need to do? What will I do to do this?" But perhaps the greatest strength of a coach is in the Q4 energy of "Okay. Now do it."

The in8model® is whole-of-brain coaching and is geared to gently adjusting a person's neurology into a fit for purpose position. It is more than systems based business consulting and more than the hyper energy yell and tell seminars, which motivate but rarely produce sustainable change.

You, as a chiropractor, take people on journeys towards freedom. You patiently walk with them as they elevate their consciousness and their vibration through the chiropractic lifestyle. But who is doing that for you and for your business?

I attribute my joyful and prosperous journey of over 50 years in the chiropractic profession to taking good advice from those who had trod the path before me and being held accountable by my coaches.

The Attractive Practice Model is the natural result of everything we live, teach and coach at Quest Chiropractic Coaching. We are a resource for Chiropractors and their teams who are engaged in and committed to doing what makes their heart sing, changing the world and making a profit.

The program has a home for practice owners, associates and CAs, creating more attraction, more nurture, more delivery and greater expansion for their business and the people they serve.

If you are at a stage where you would like support and challenge from a team and community that care about your success, respect your philosophy and are prepared to help you say yes to, and be accountable for your potential then book a brief Clarity call.

Playtime

- Book a Clarity Call with us.

About the Author

Hi, I am Mark Postles. I have a profound curiosity for life, for human beings and for understanding how they tick.

I love mastering my skills as an inspirational communicator and enjoy bringing out the best in people, teams, and organizations. As a professional speaker, business coach, professional development expert, chiropractor and author, I aim to touch people's lives with my vision for humanity.

My life purpose is to integrate the big picture of possibilities with the practical details and realities of life, relationships and business, thus generating sustainable change for our planet.

I would love to hear from you. If you wish to access our innovative coaching programs our details are below:

mark@questchiropracticcoaching.com

www.questchiropracticcoaching.com

mark@thein8model.com

www.thein8model.com

Acknowledgements

Credits and acknowledgments are so difficult to quantify. There have been daily pivotal moments, blinding flashes of the obvious and intuitive epiphanies that have come from the most unexpected and many times, mundane and even negative experiences.

I am grateful for all of the people who have presented in my journey of life so far. It has been, and continues to be an incredible adventure with the good and the bad, the bad in the good, the good in the bad, the ugly and beautiful, the beauty in the ugly, the ugly in the beautiful, the pain and the pleasure, the pain in the pleasure and the pleasure in the pain and so on.

Every colour and texture of every person and event in the tapestry of my life has formed this incredible adventure.

It would be remiss of me not to extend my deepest gratitude to those responsible for inspiring, guiding and coercing me through the process of creating this book. Specifically, I thank my lovely wife, Jackie and my, forever questioning kids, Jason, Stefan and Ali plus our six grandchildren who are wise beyond their years. To our amazing Quest Pilots, Greg, Karen, Emma, Nimrod and Andrew. Thanks for your willingness to always challenge me. To Nerida, Clare, Janet and Eula who made sure the context, the text and the layout were fit for purpose.

They say it takes a community to raise a child; I know it's taken a community to raise this book! Thank you to the thousands of people who I have been privileged to learn from.

Here's the link and the big QR Code to the resource section for this book

https://www.questchiropracticcoaching.com/the-attractive-practice-model-resources/

Love,
Mark

www.ingramcontent.com/pod-product-compliance
Lightning Source LLC
Chambersburg PA
CBHW071550210326
41597CB00019B/3183